THE PICTURE BOOK OF

CHURCHES

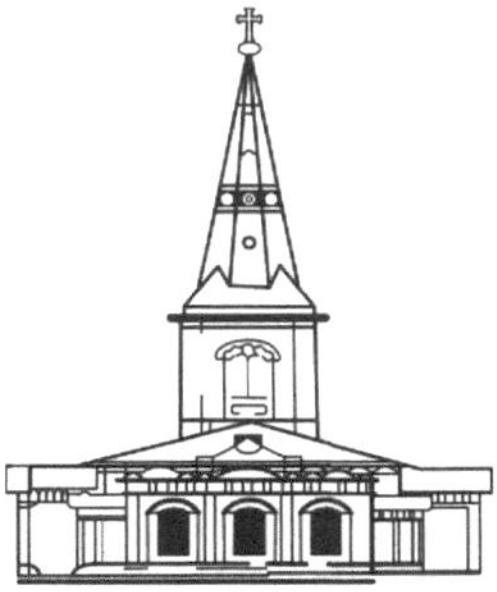

SUNNY STREET
BOOKS

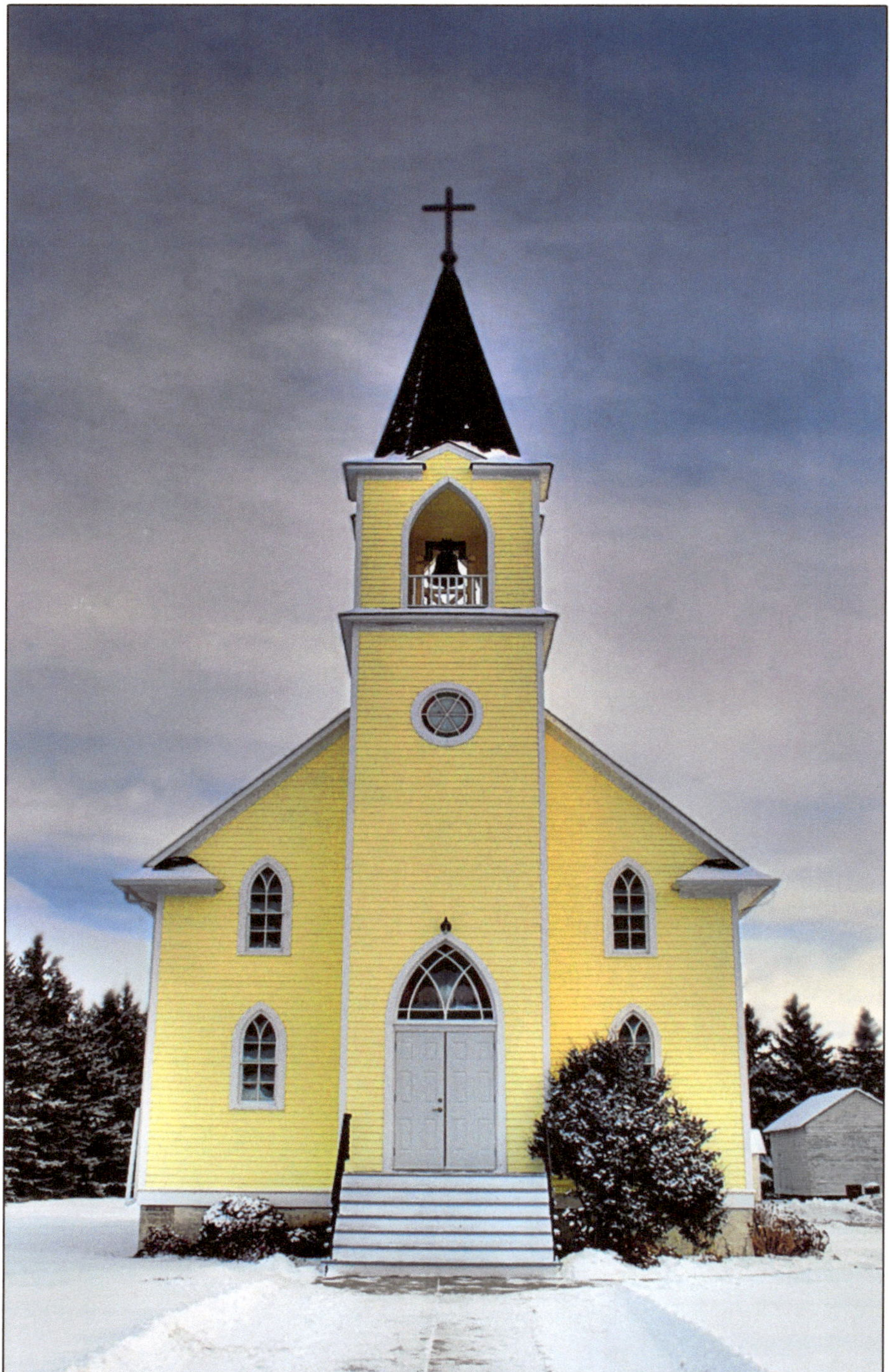

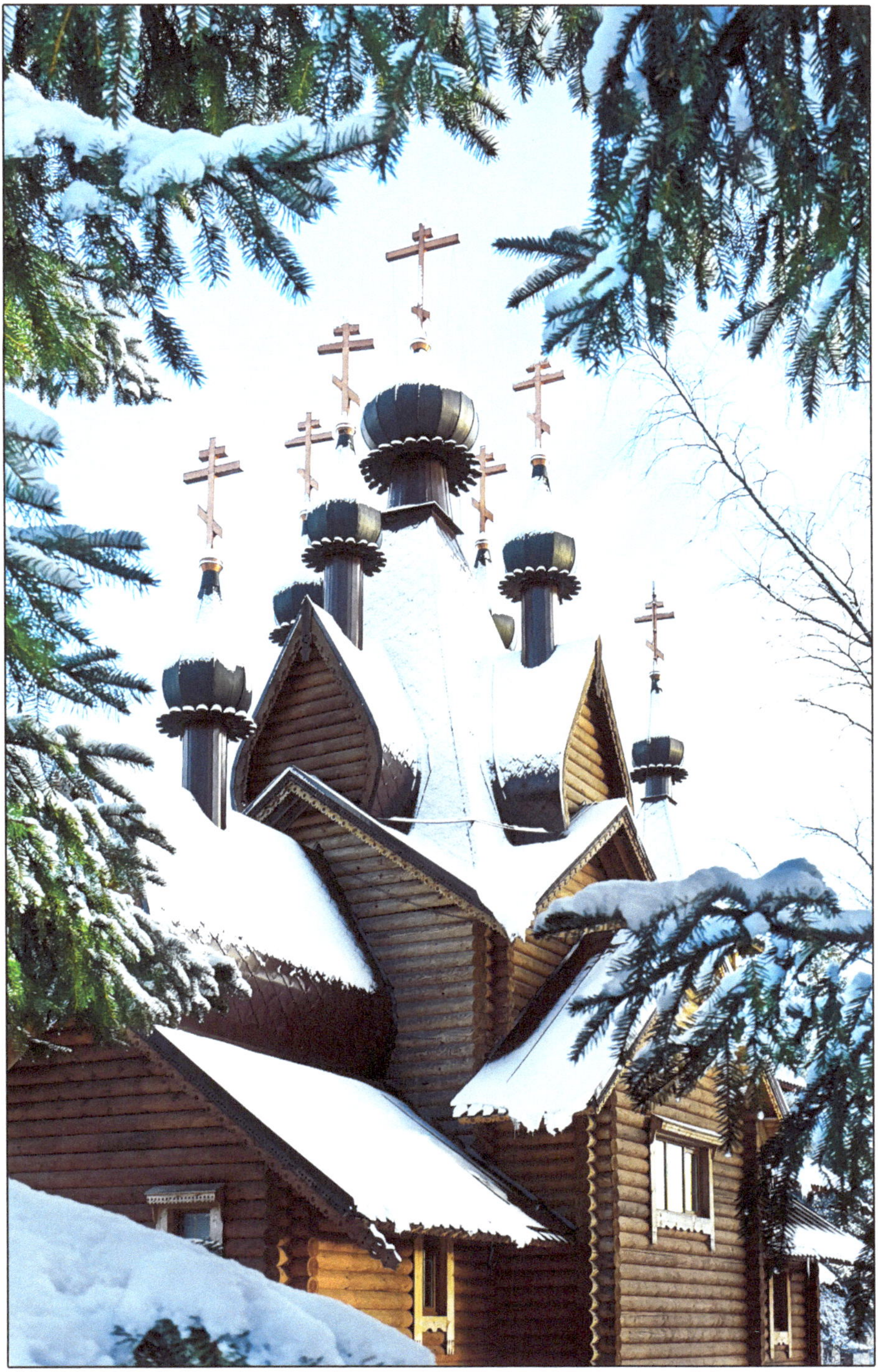

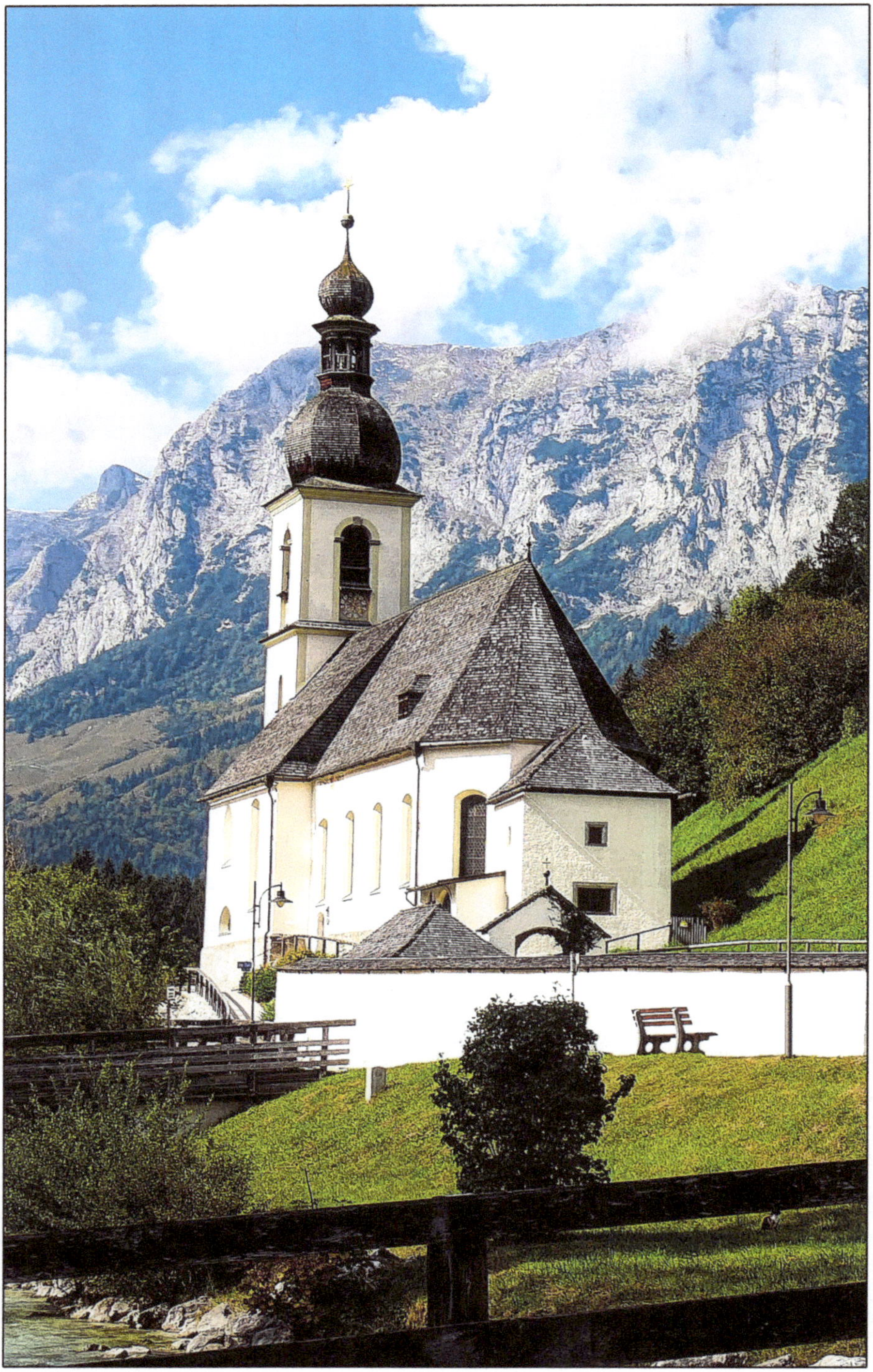

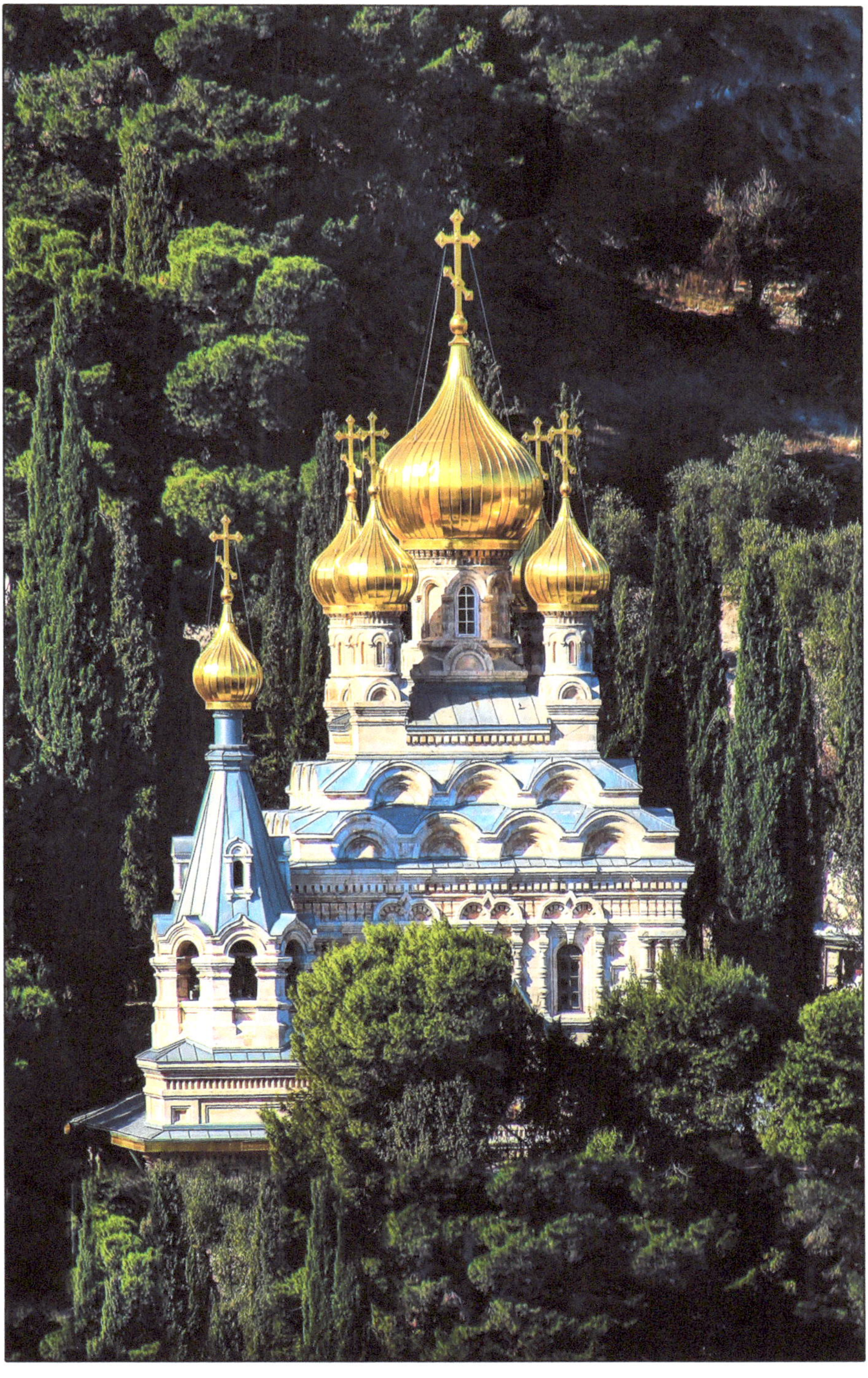

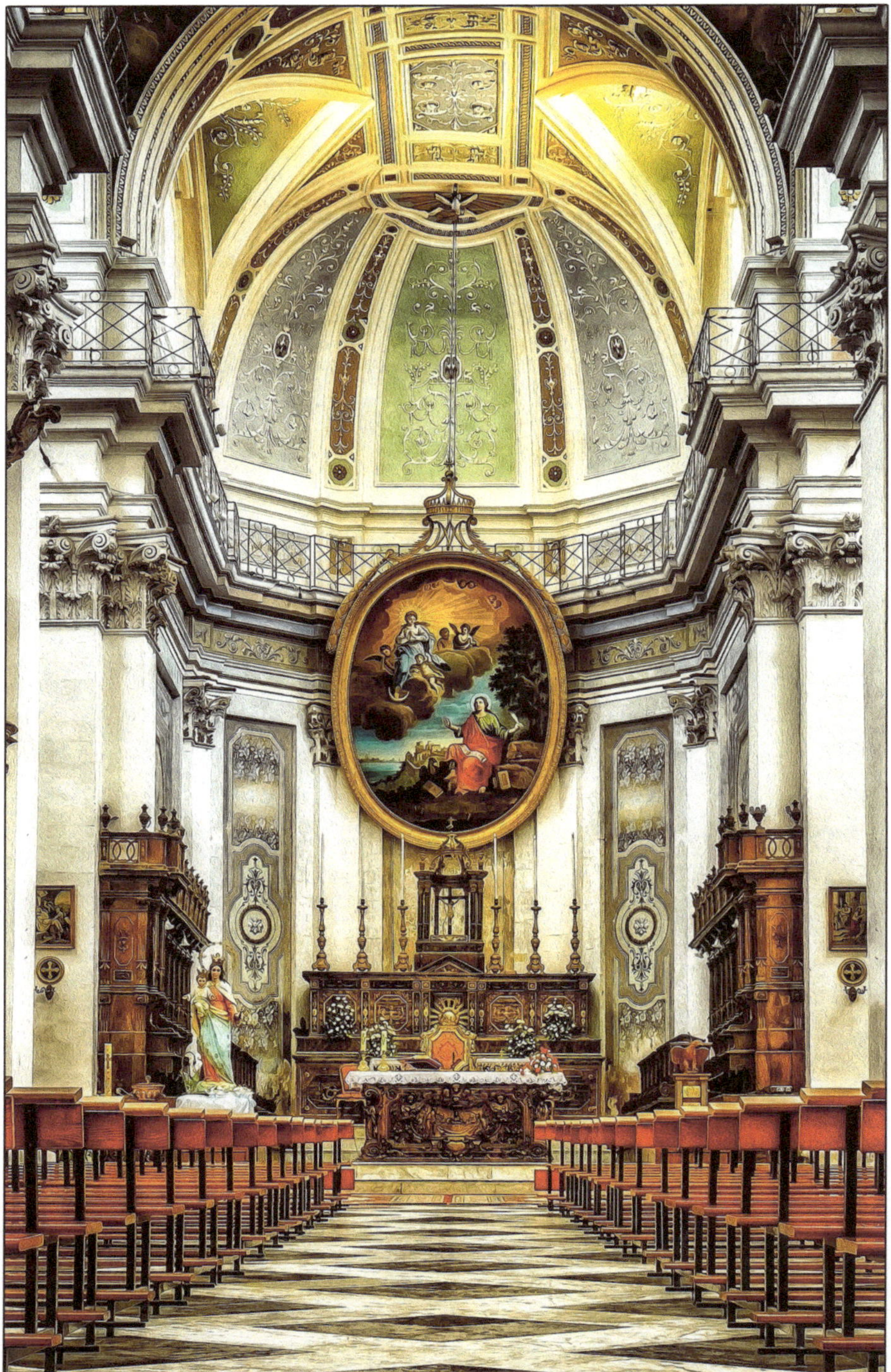

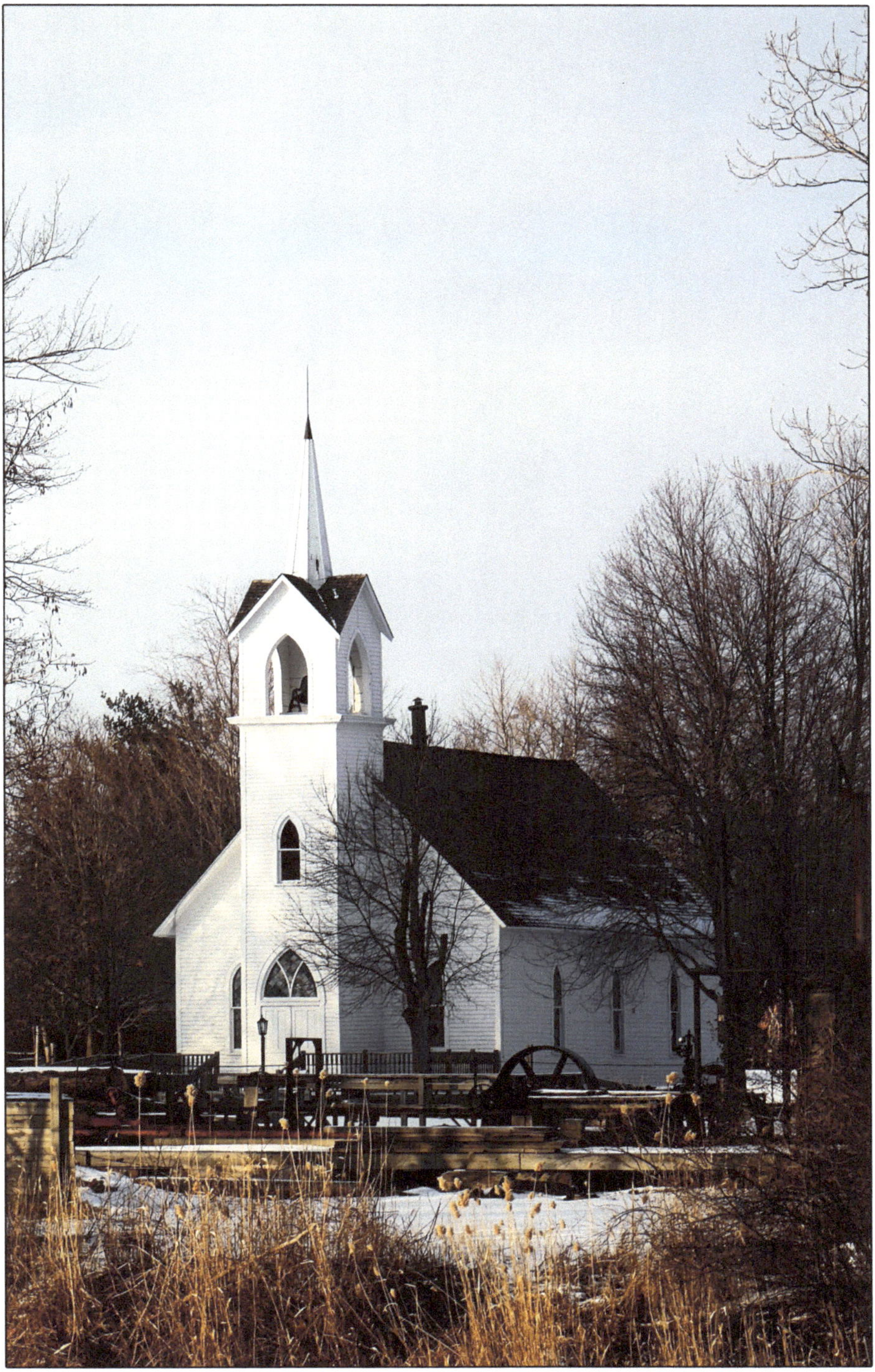

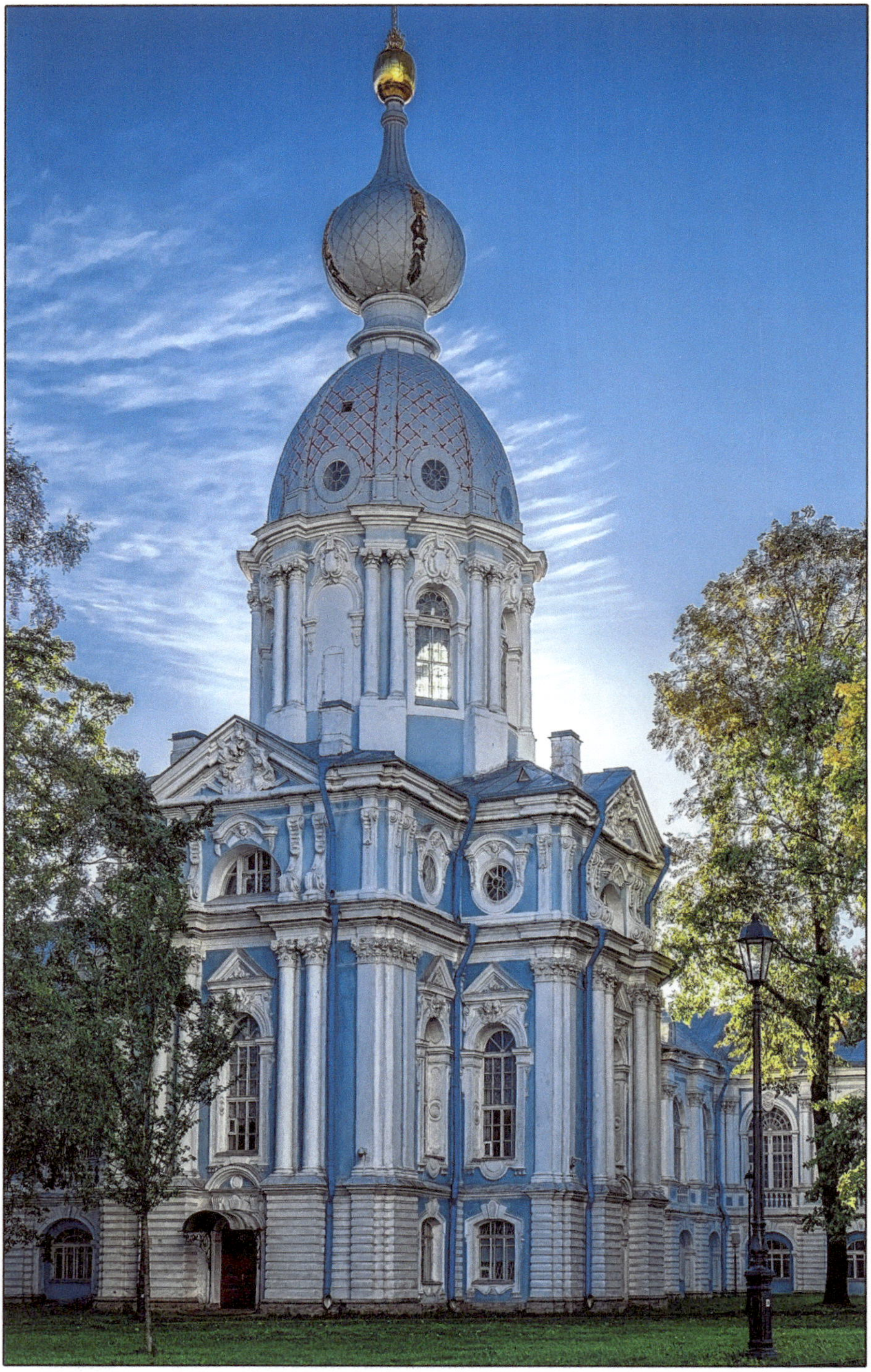

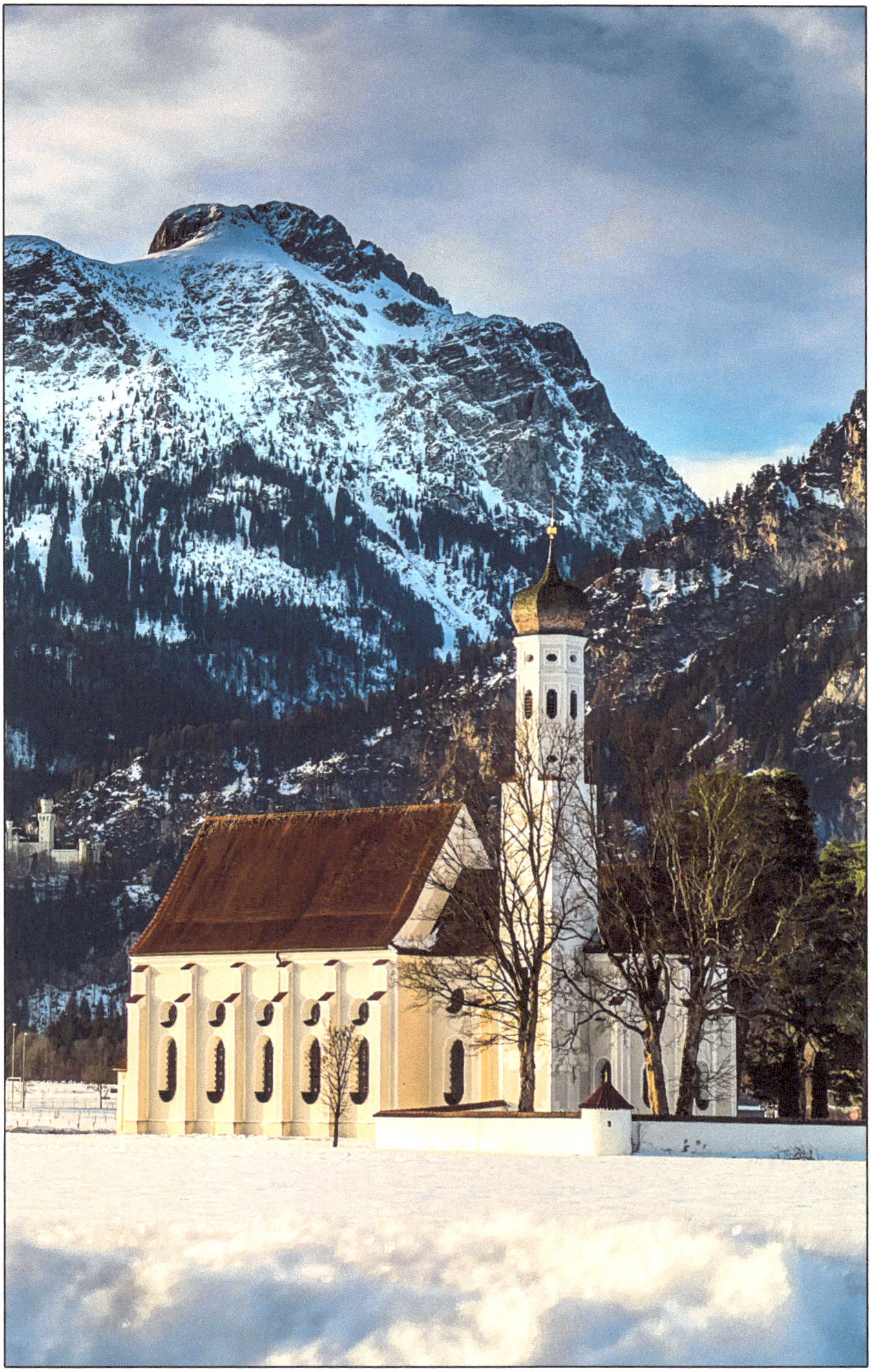

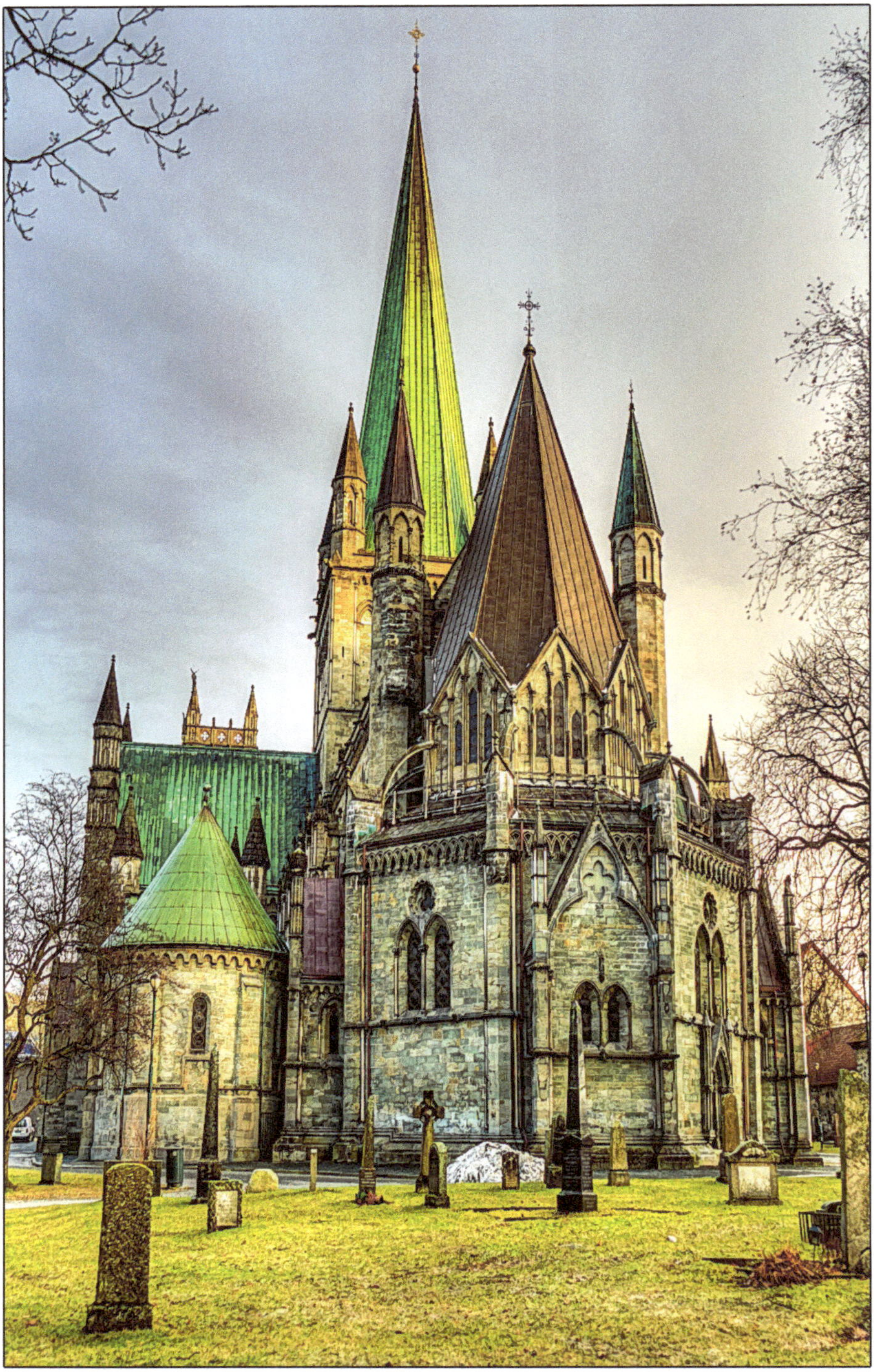

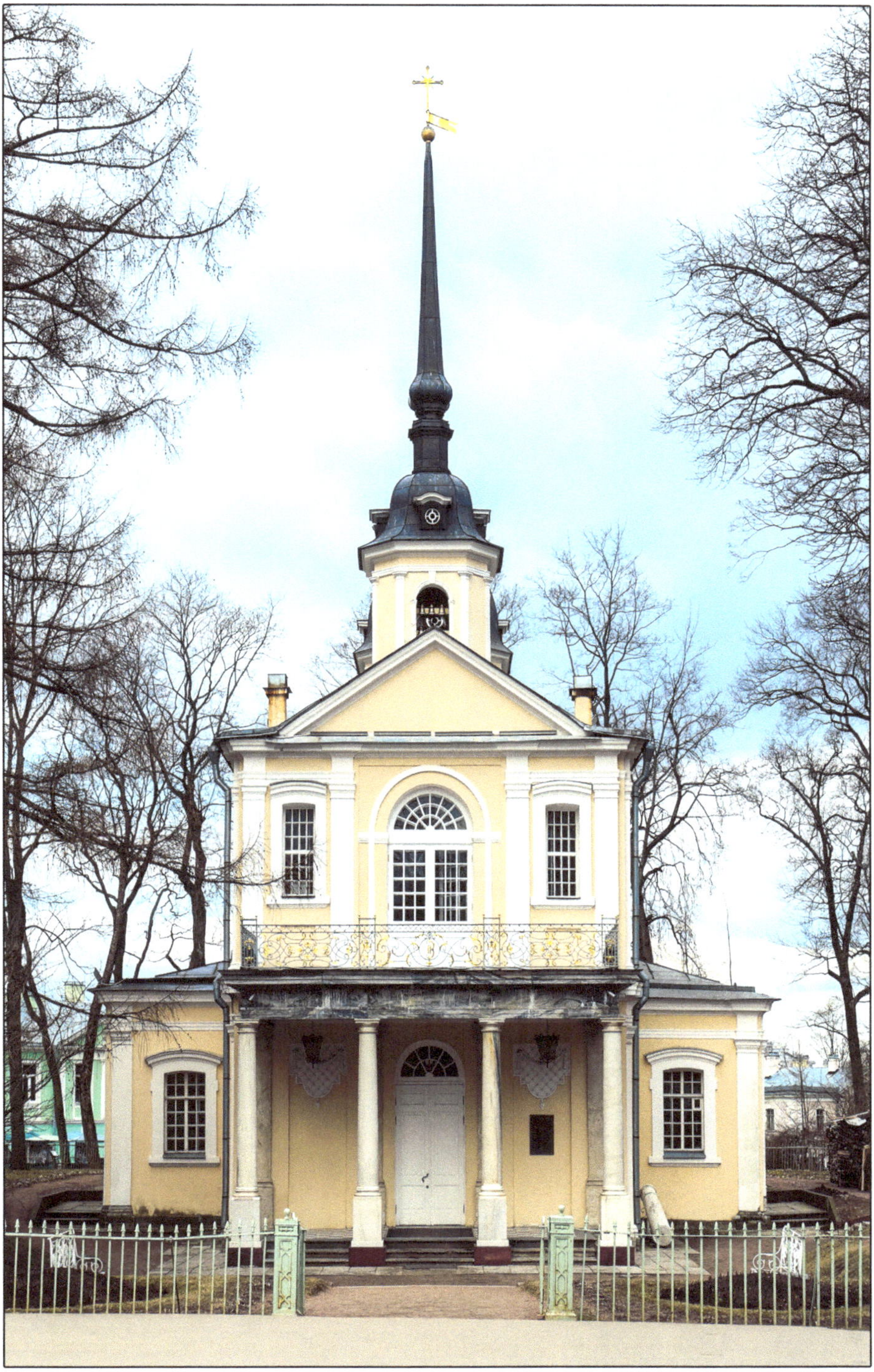

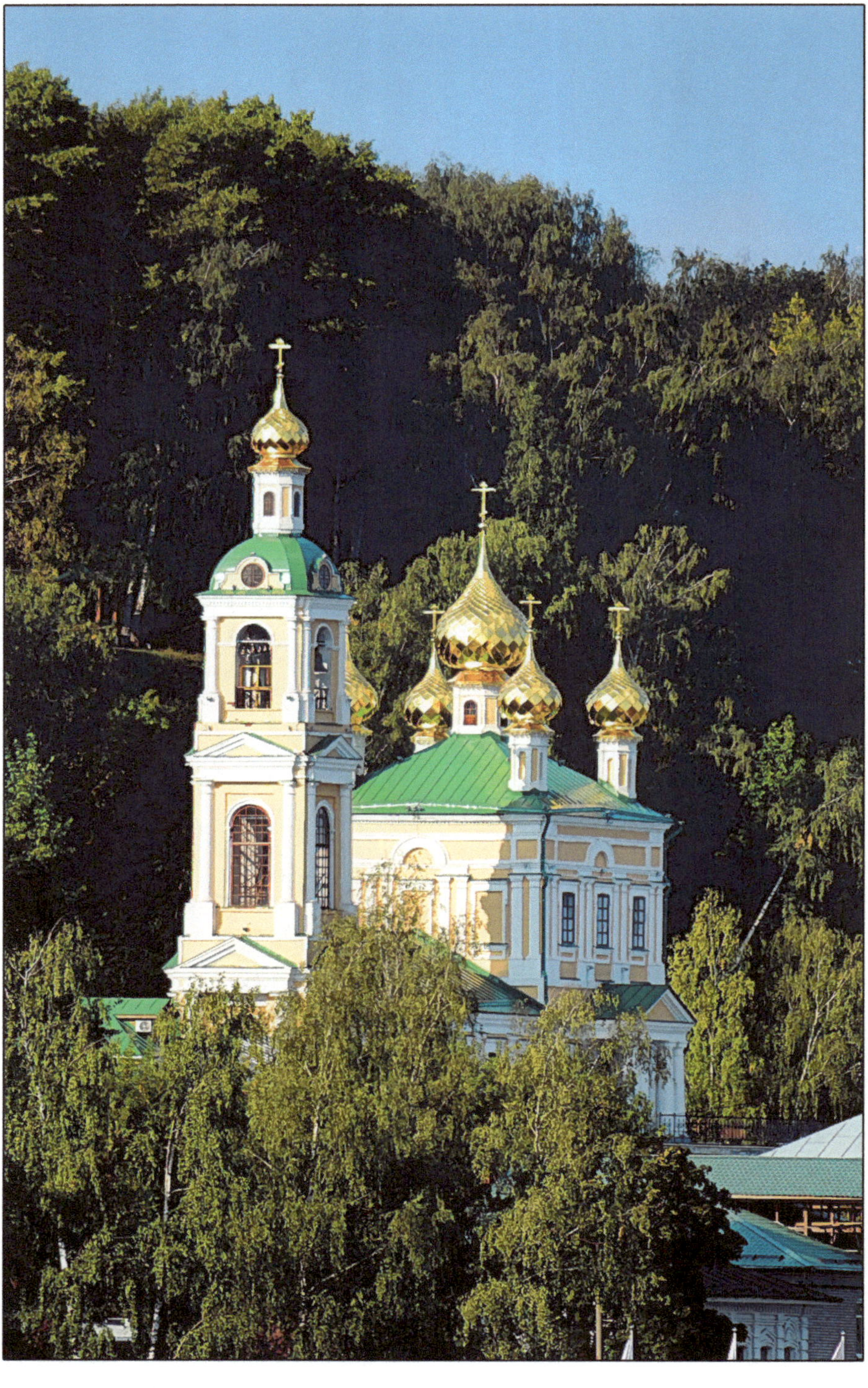

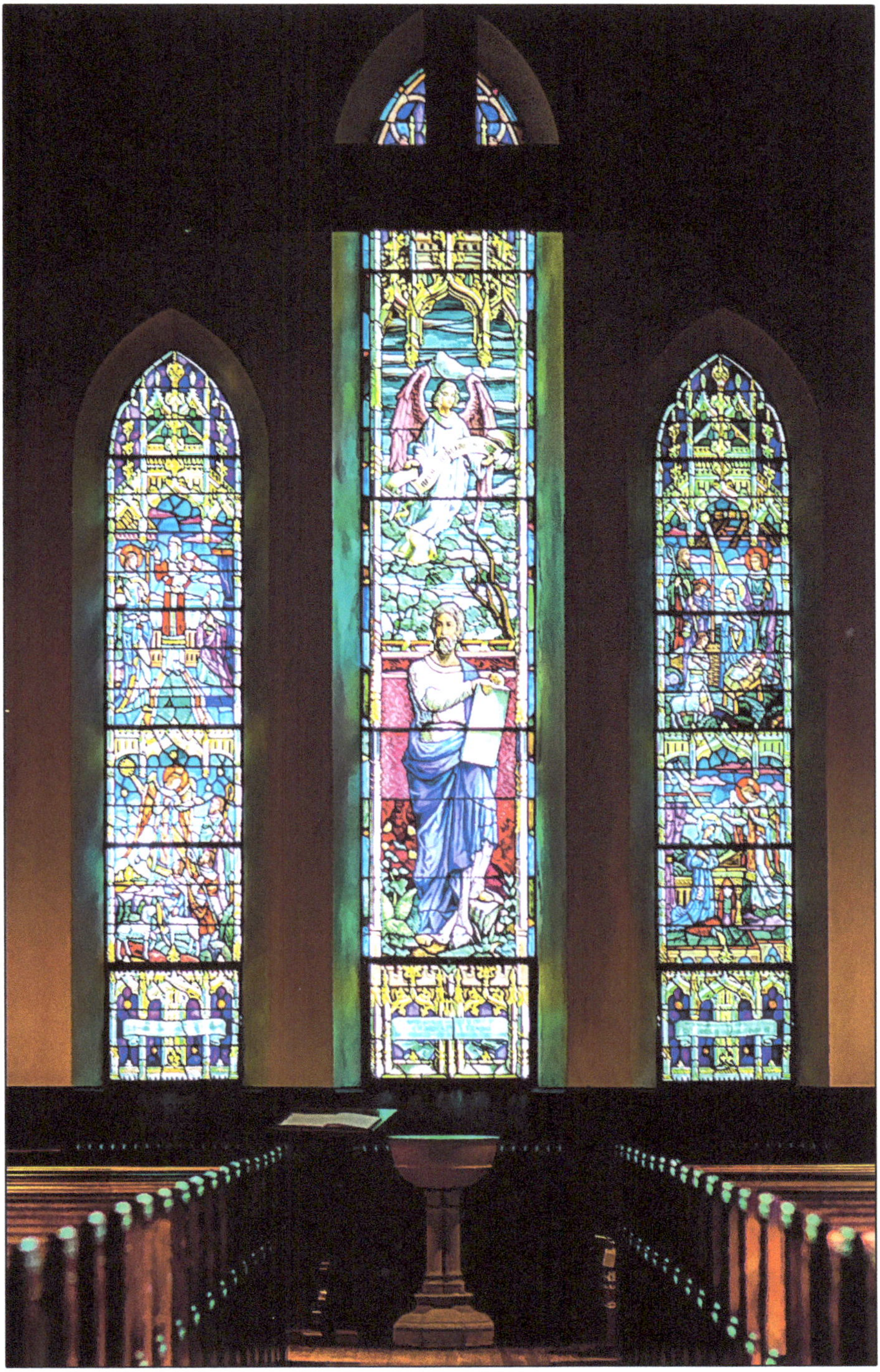

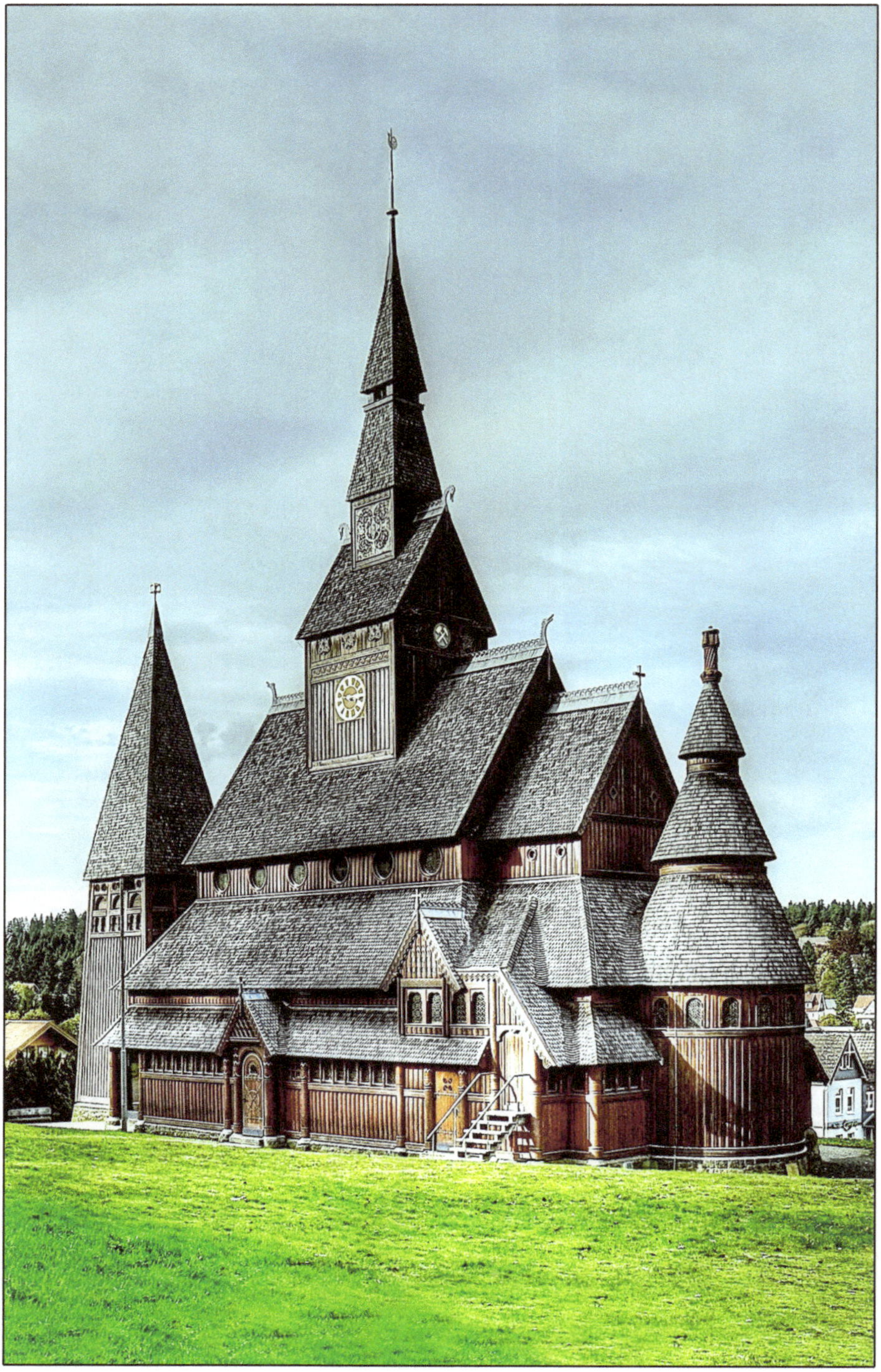

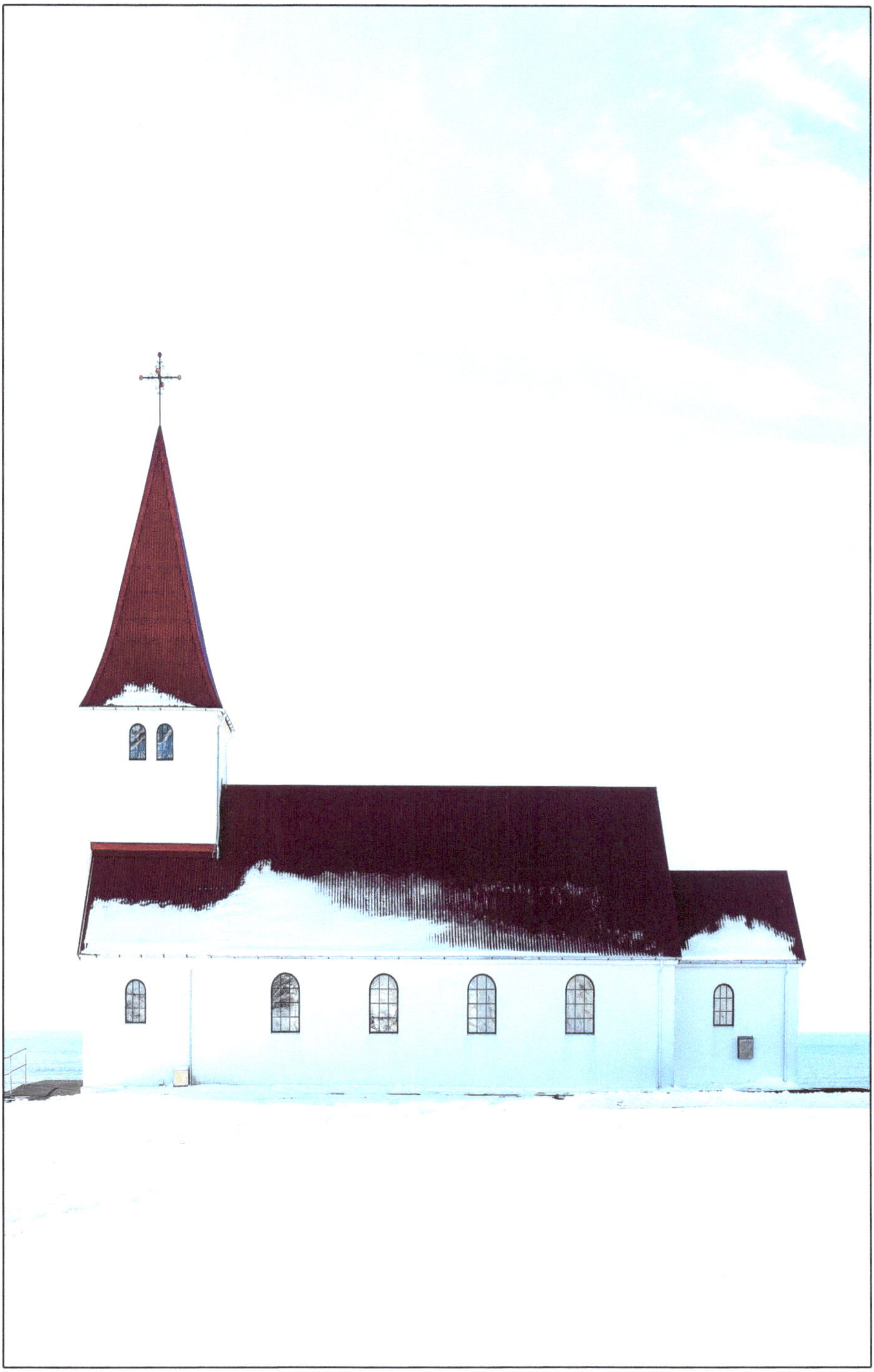

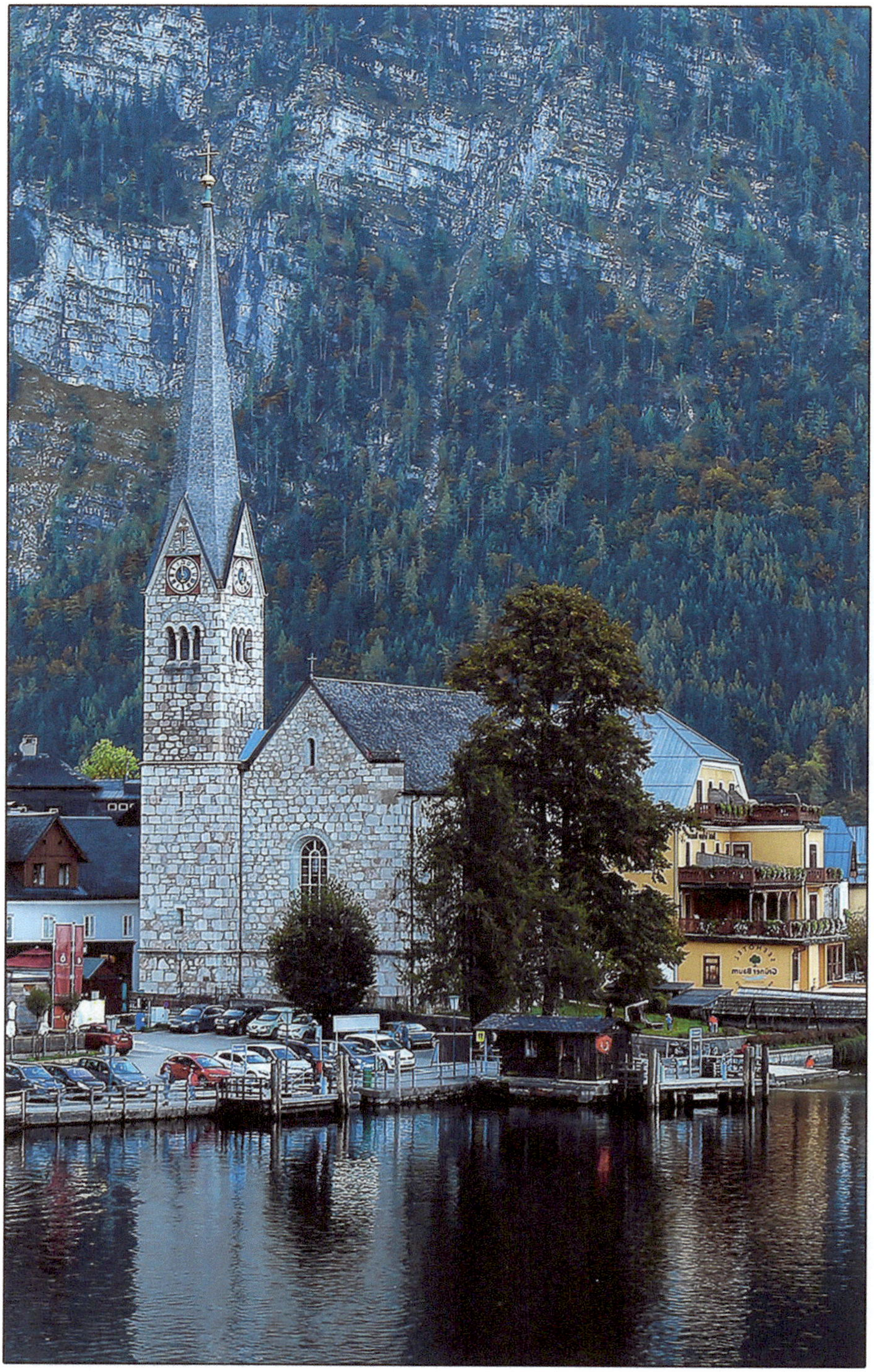

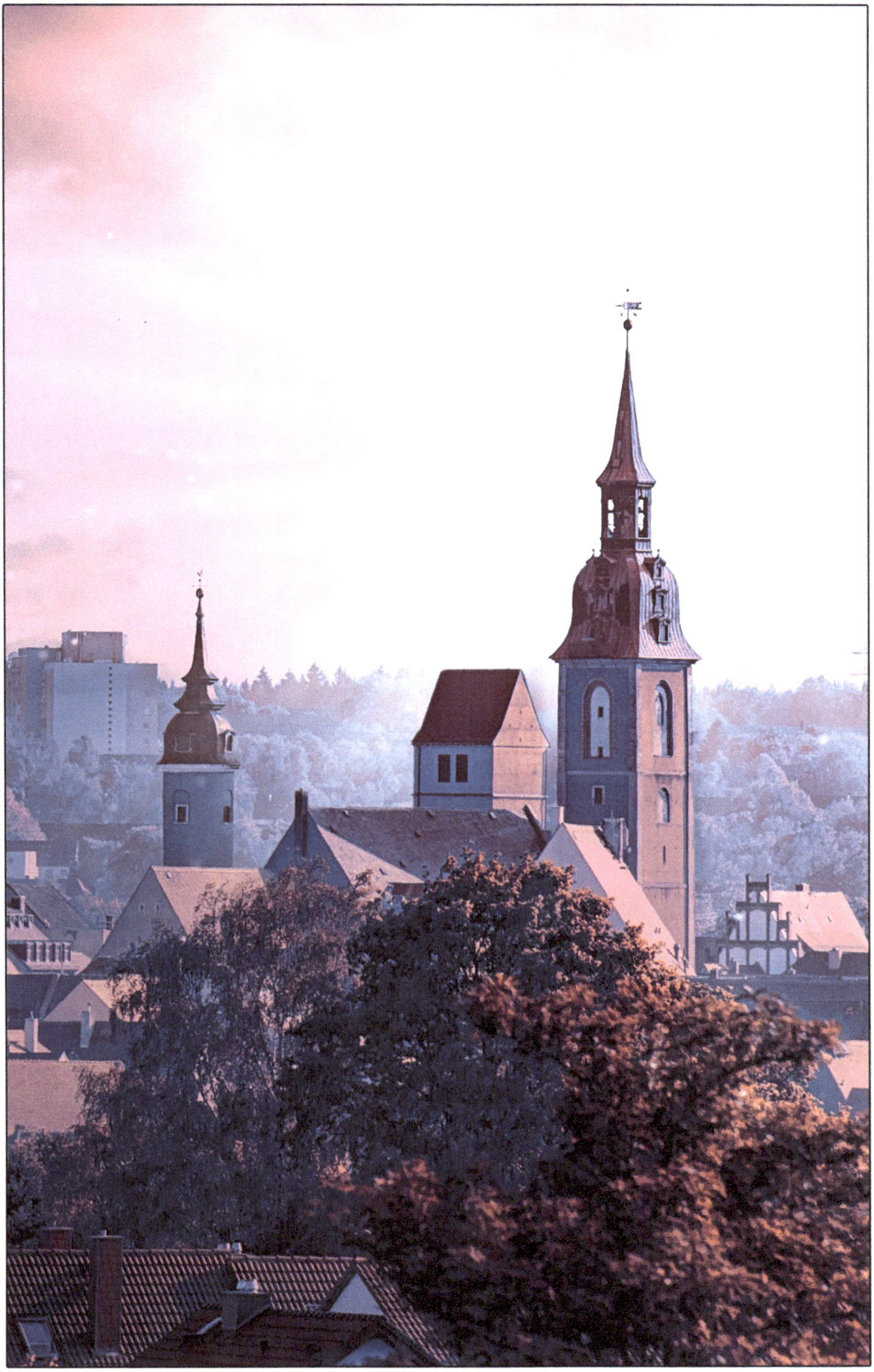

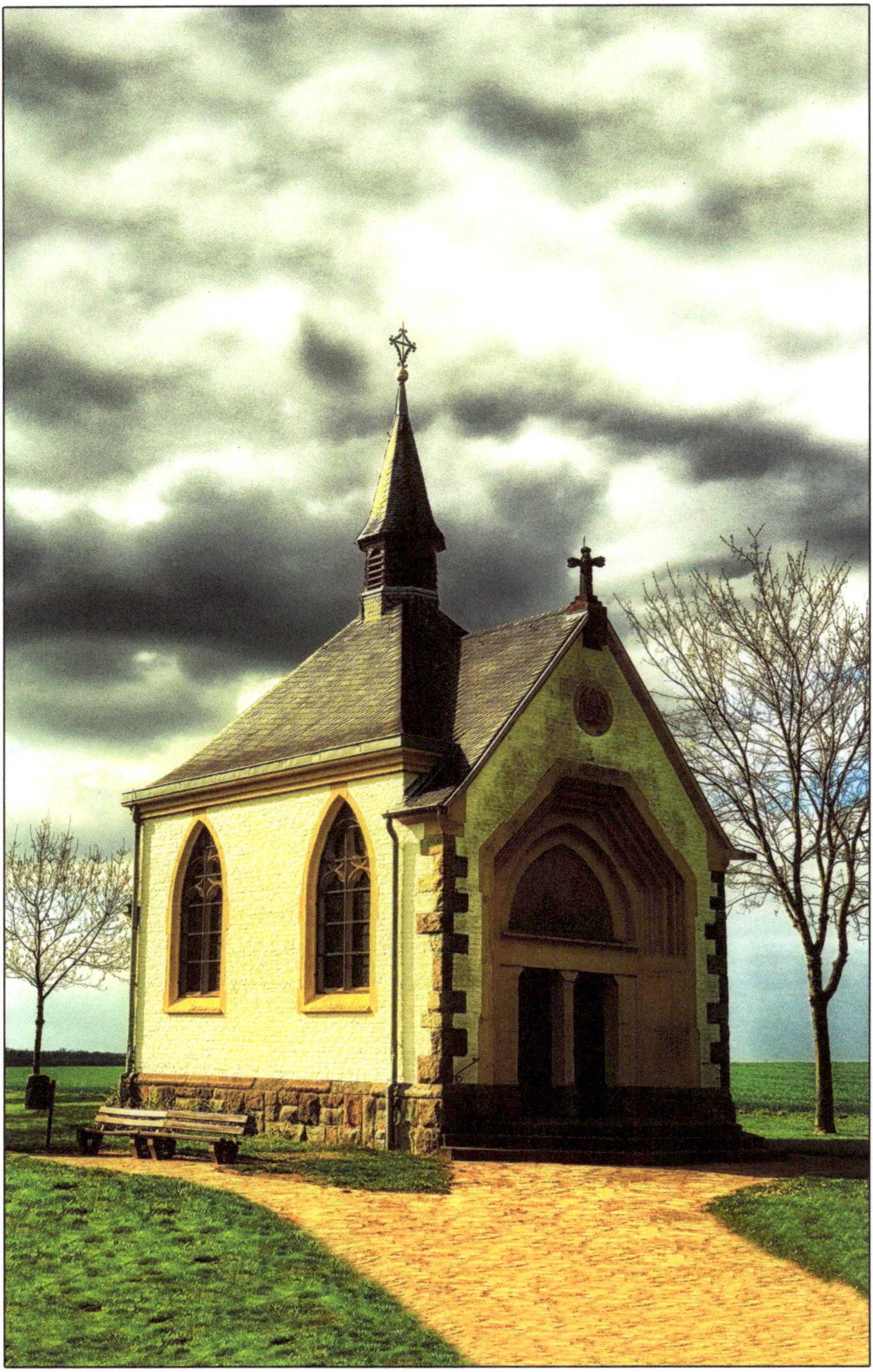

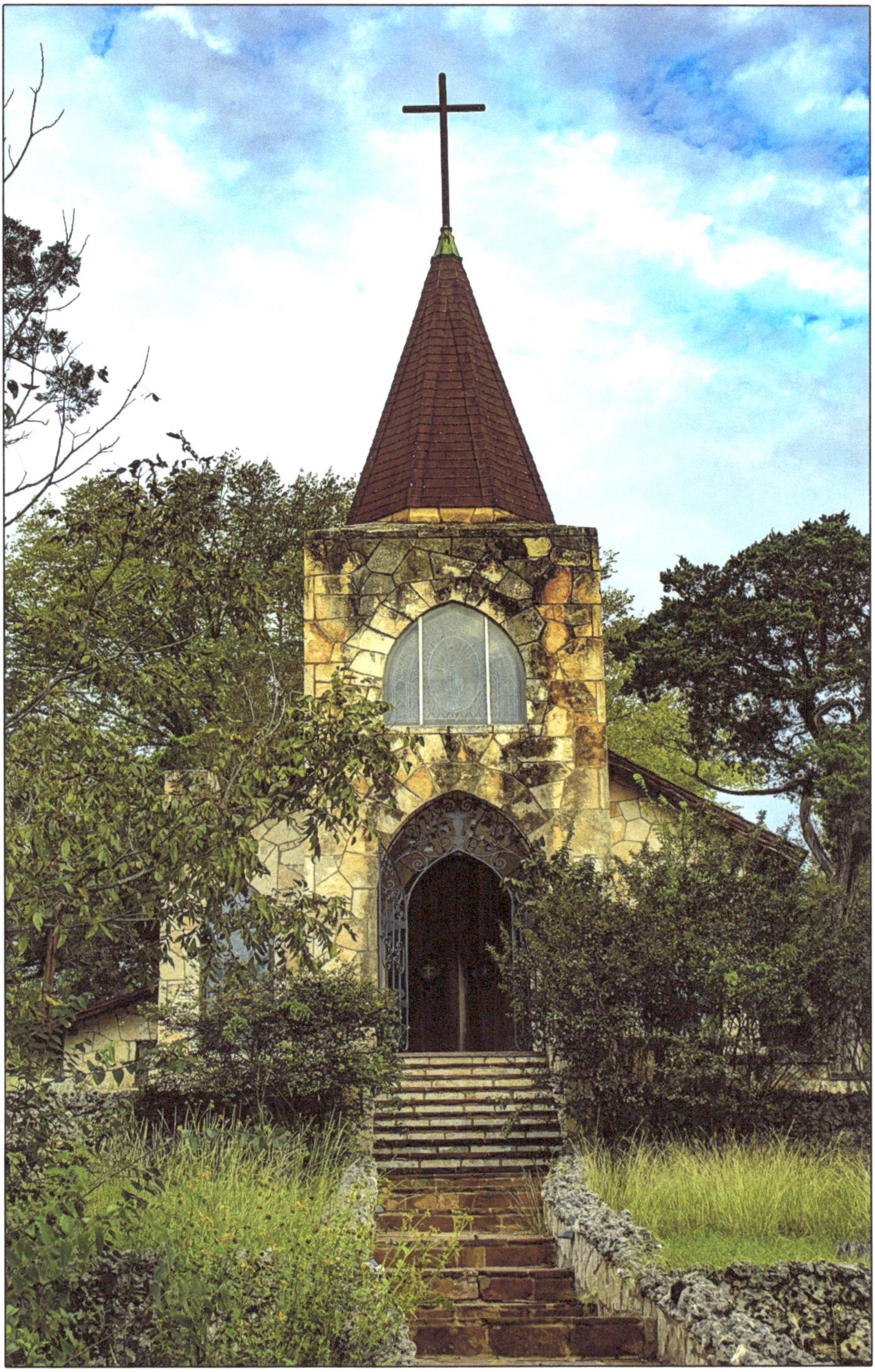

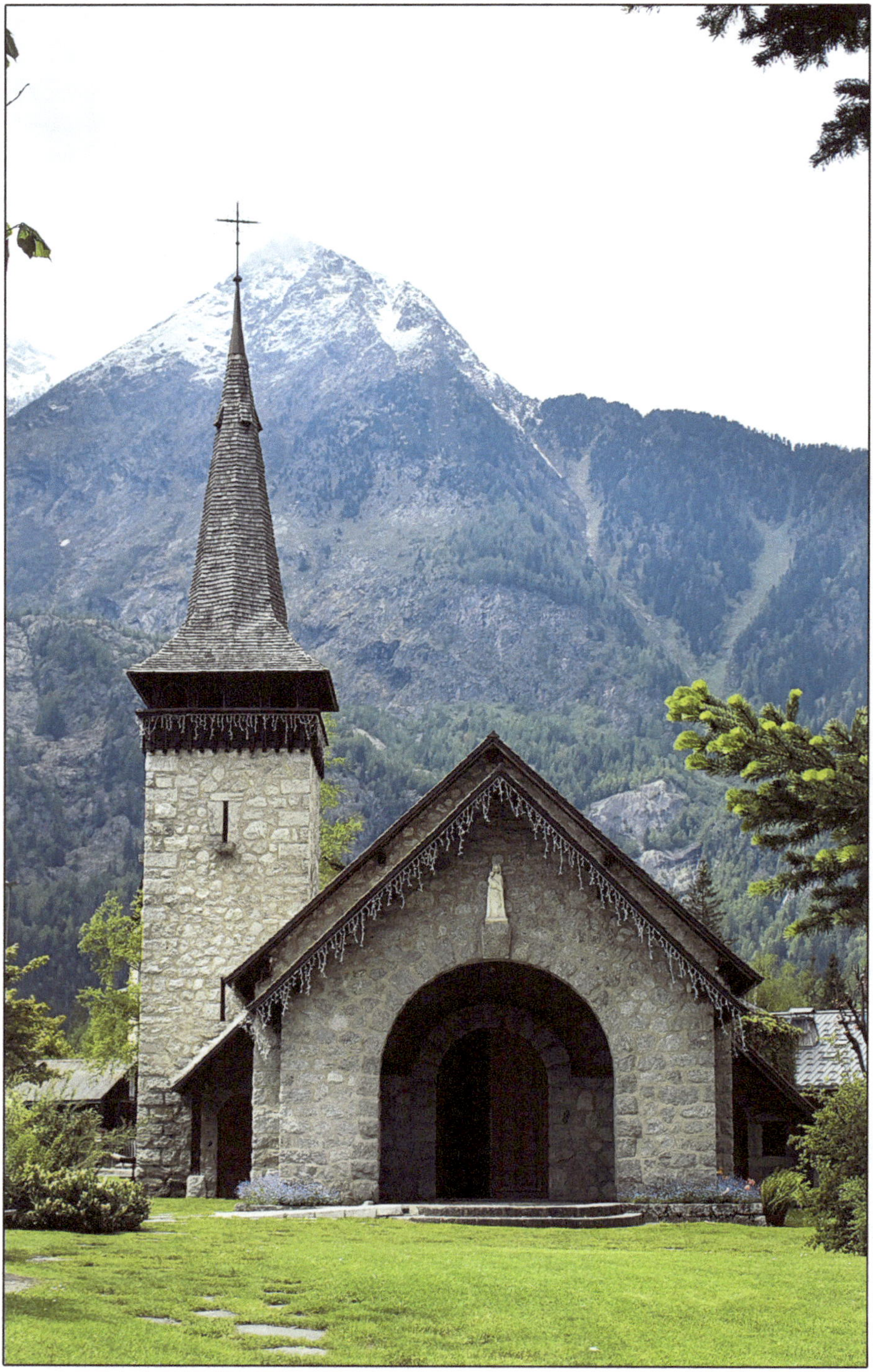

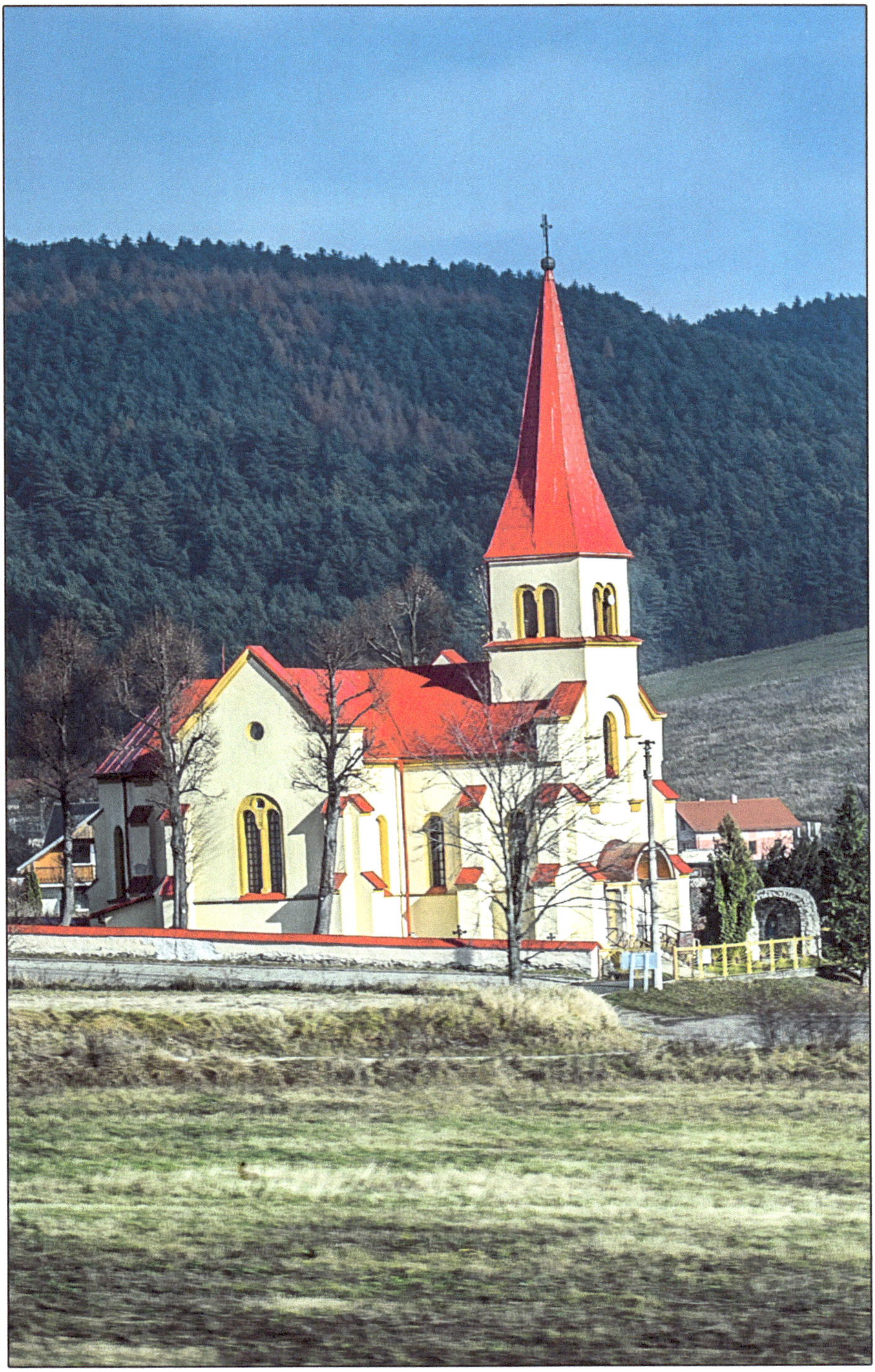

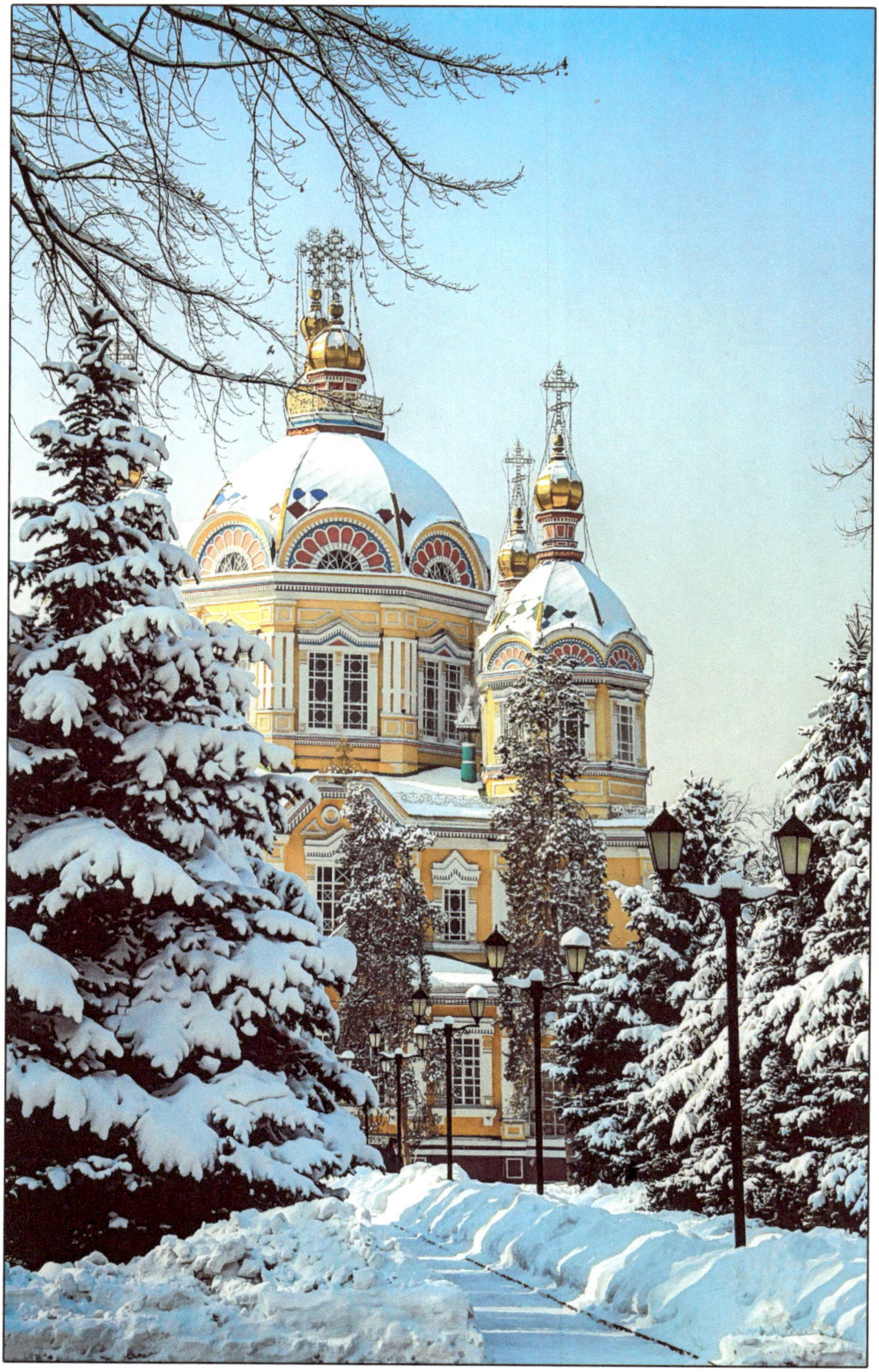

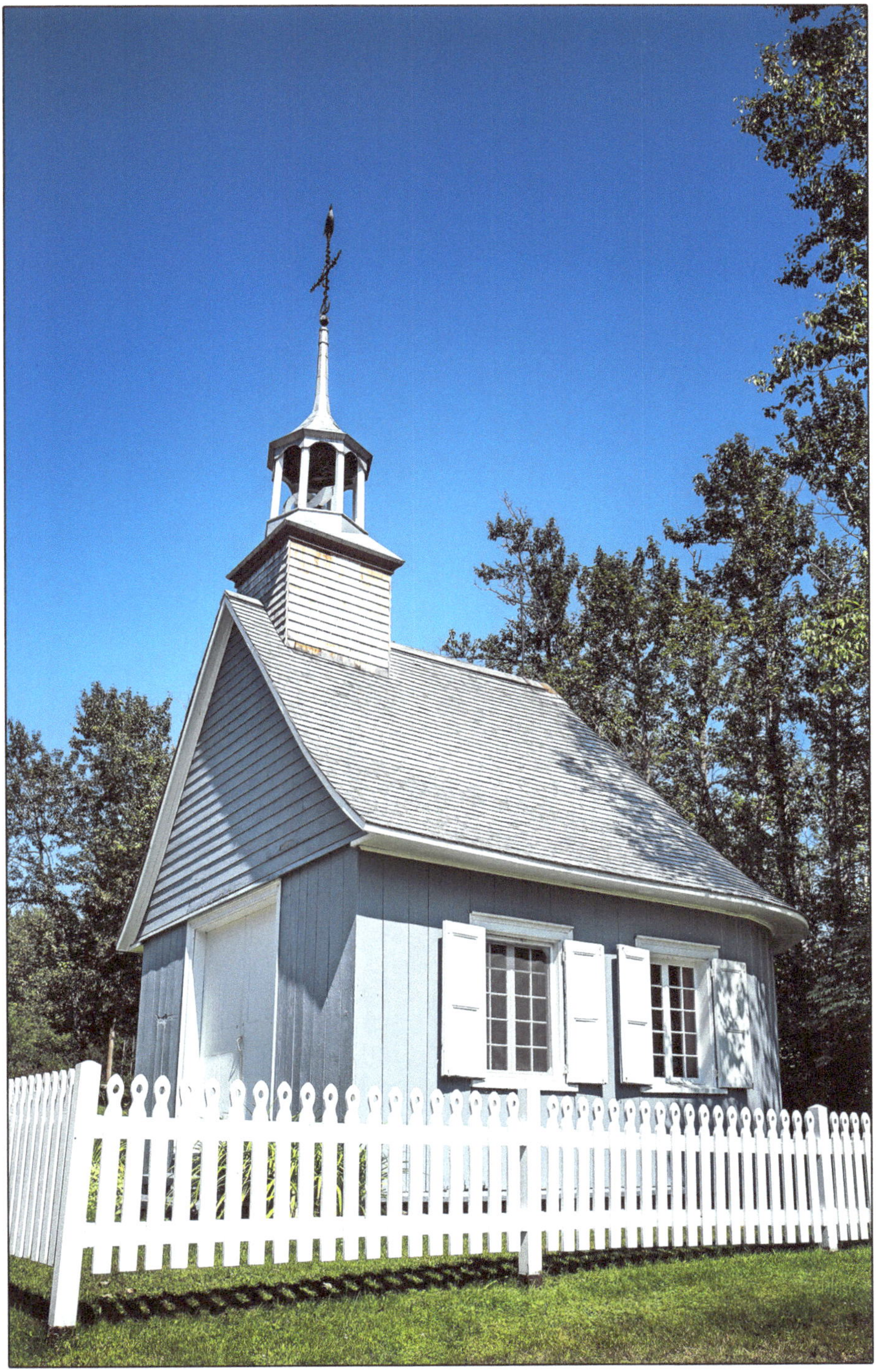

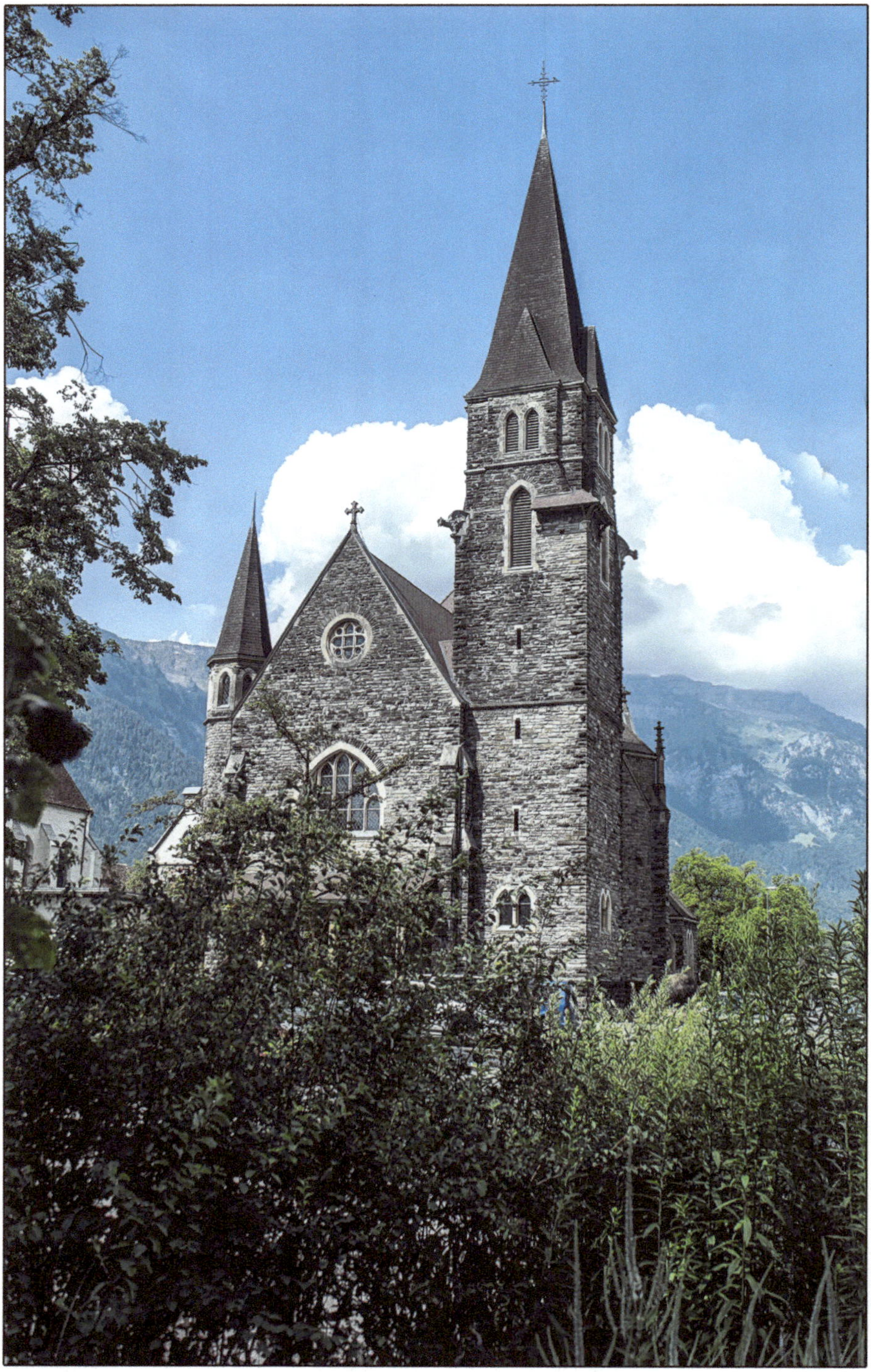

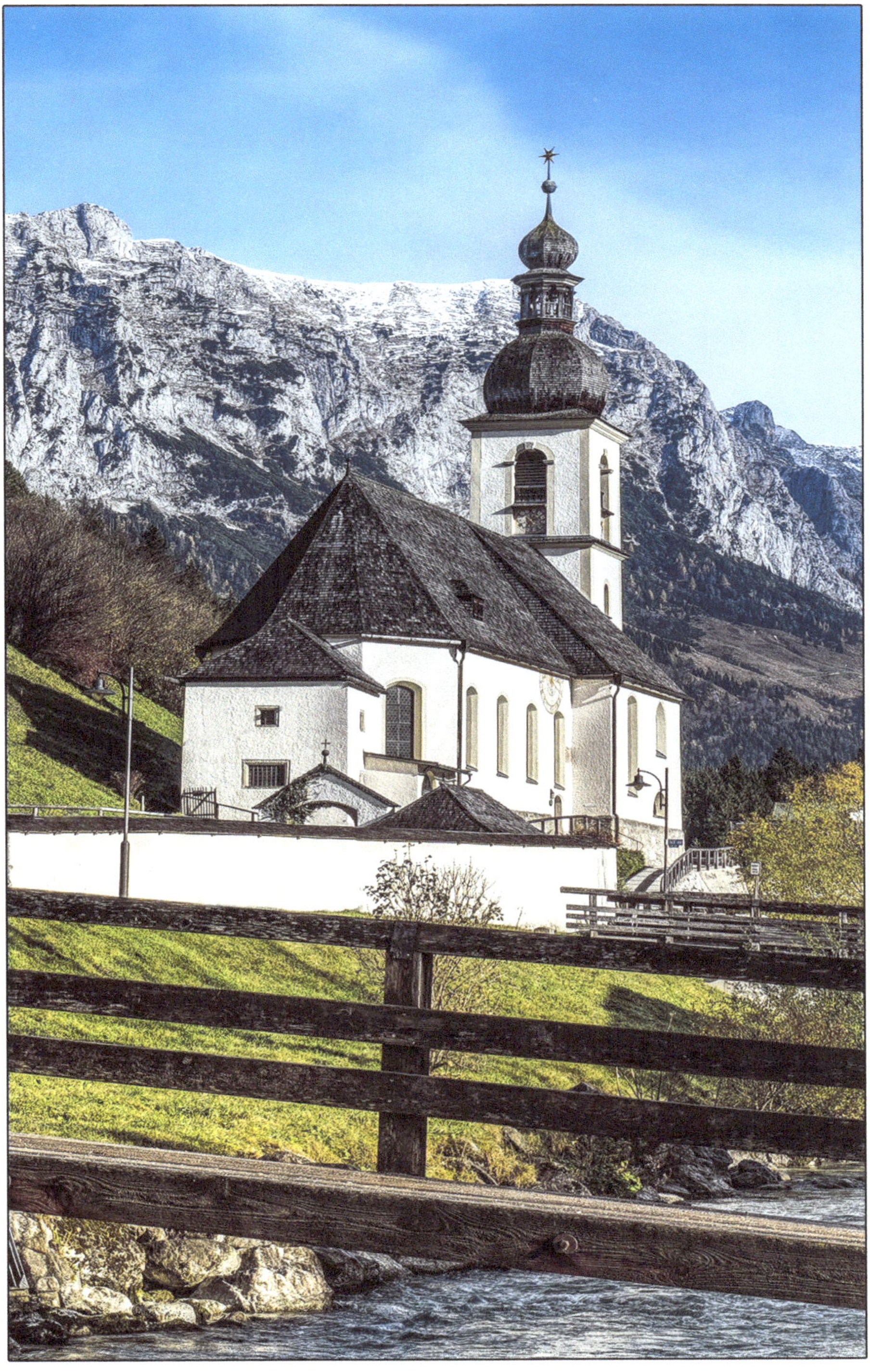

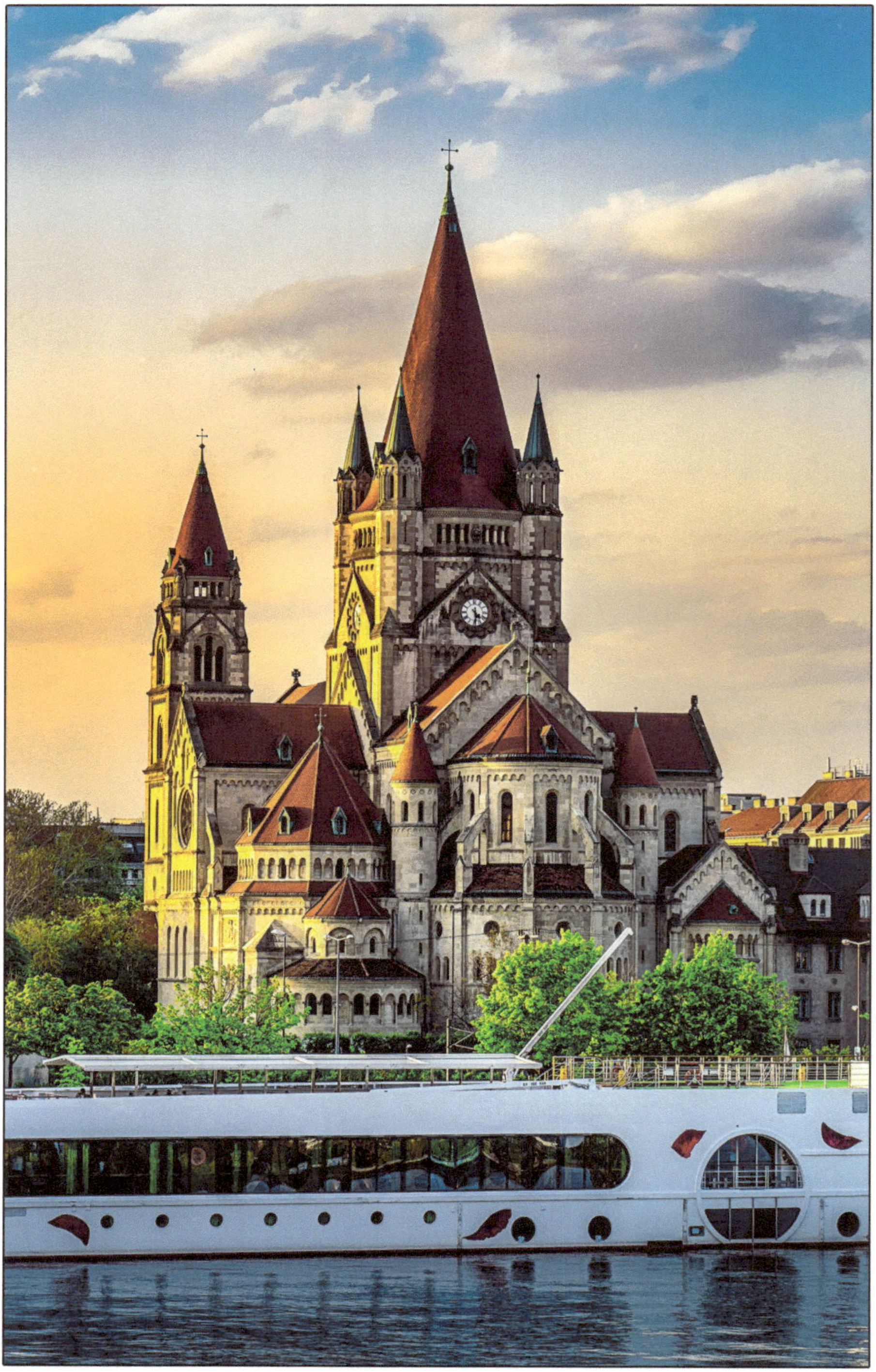

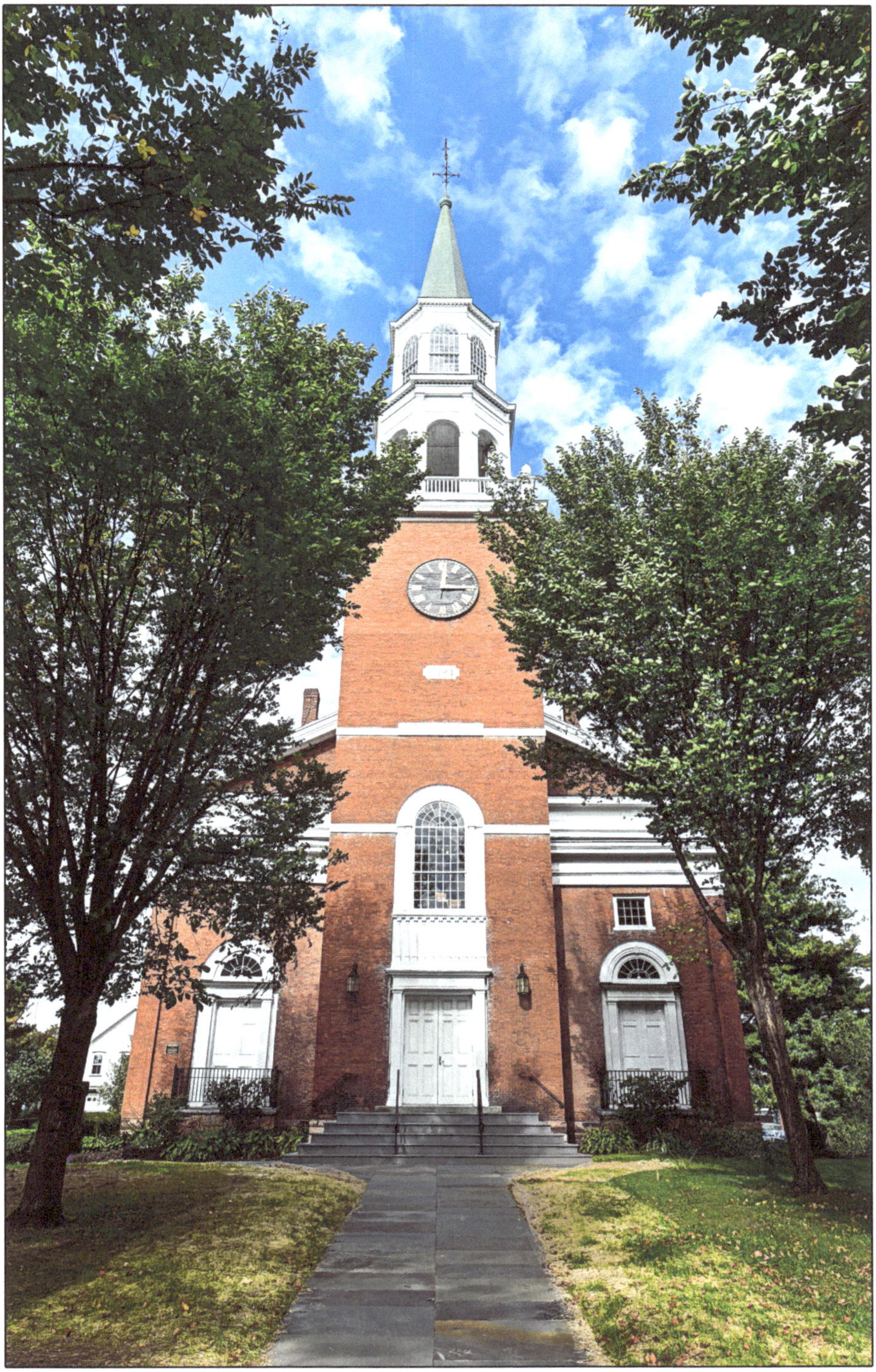

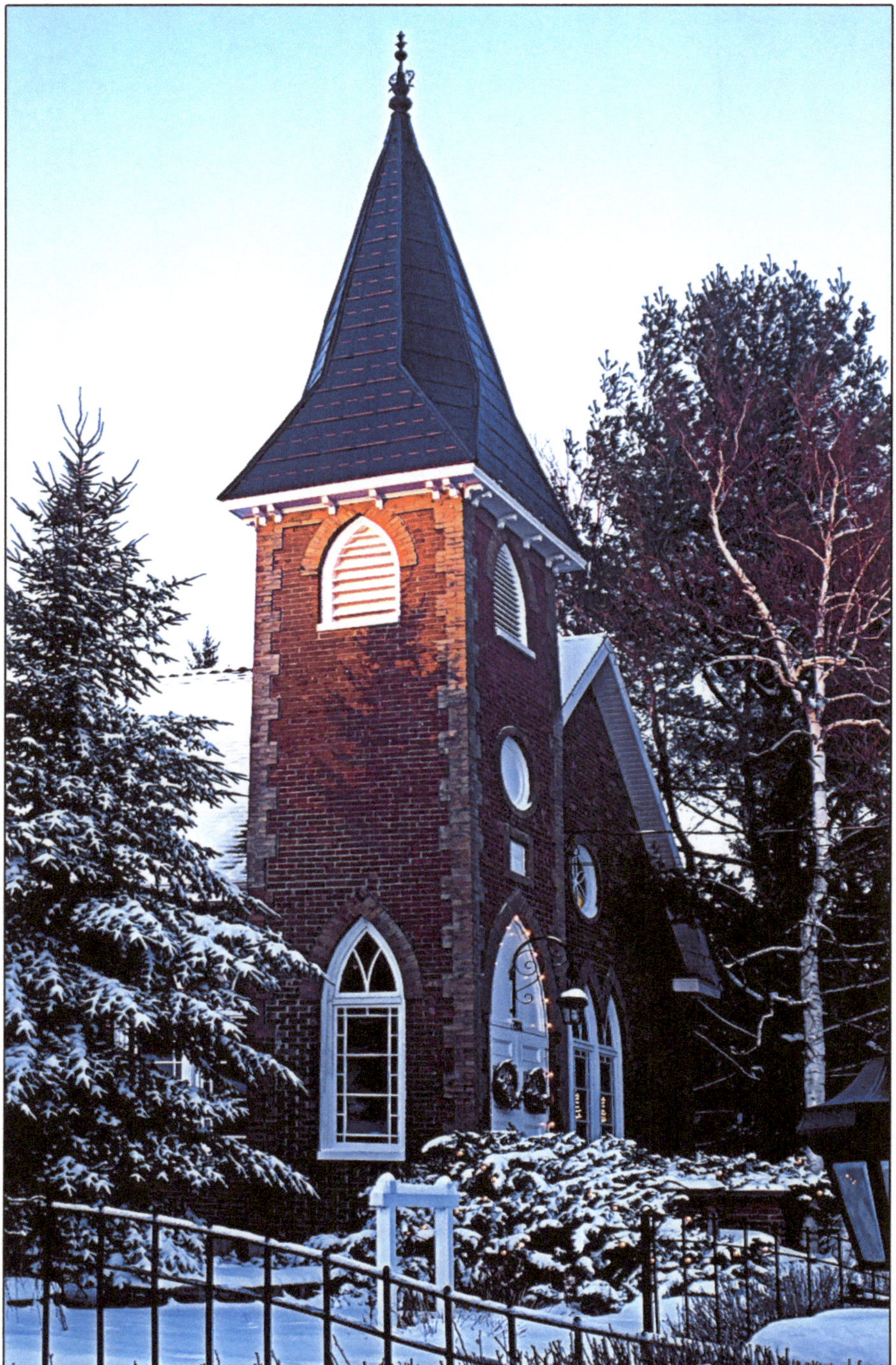

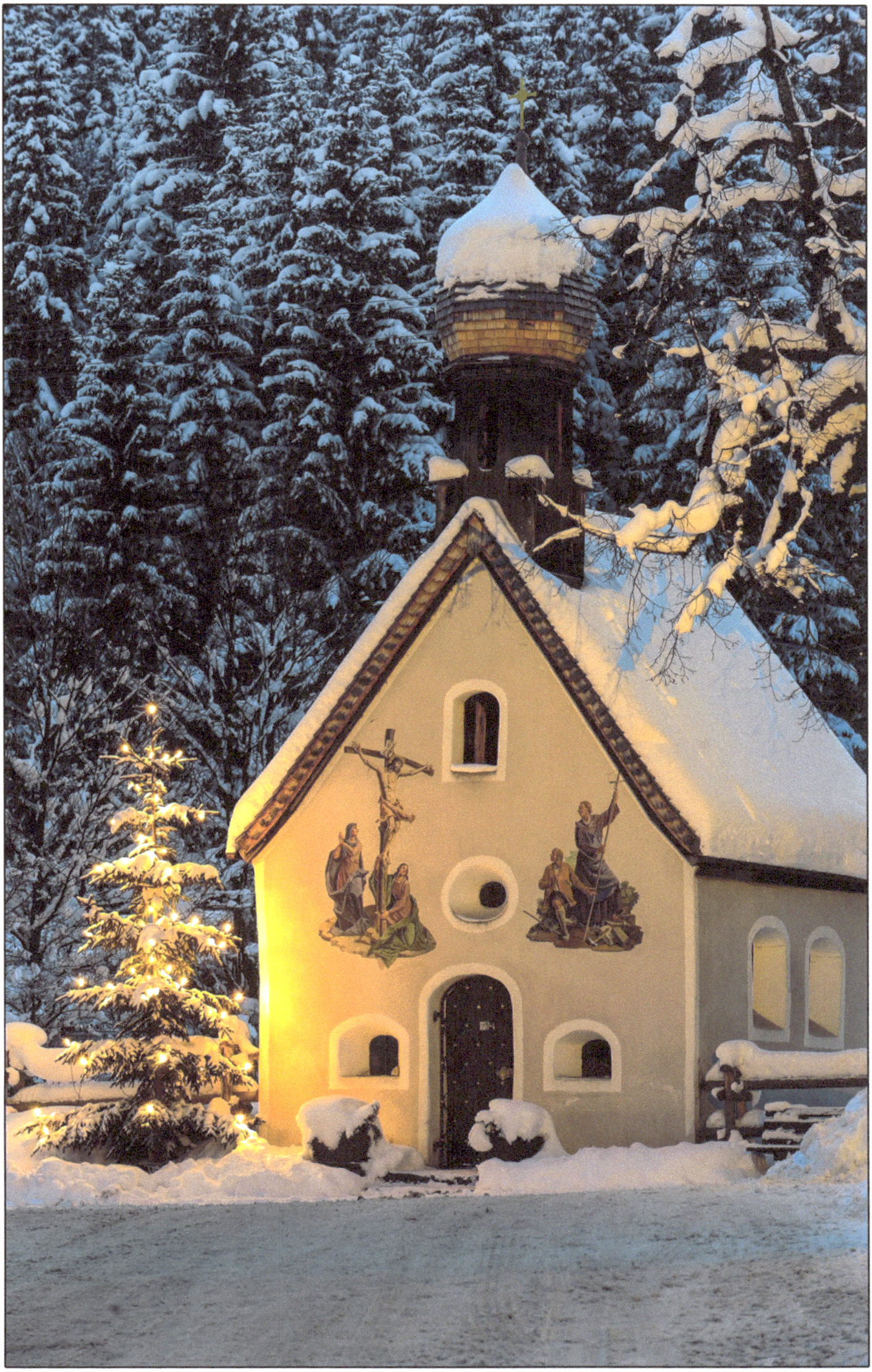

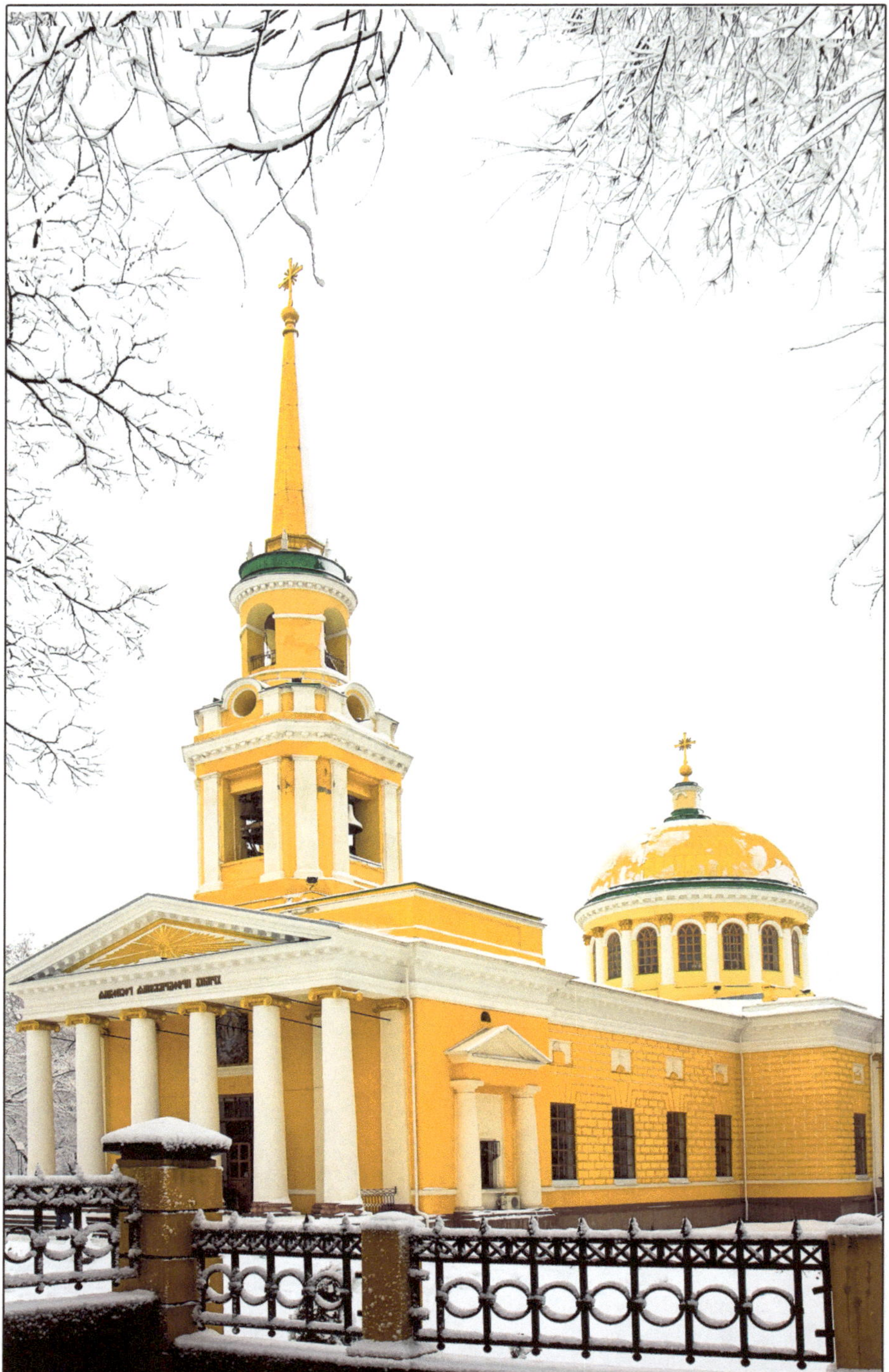

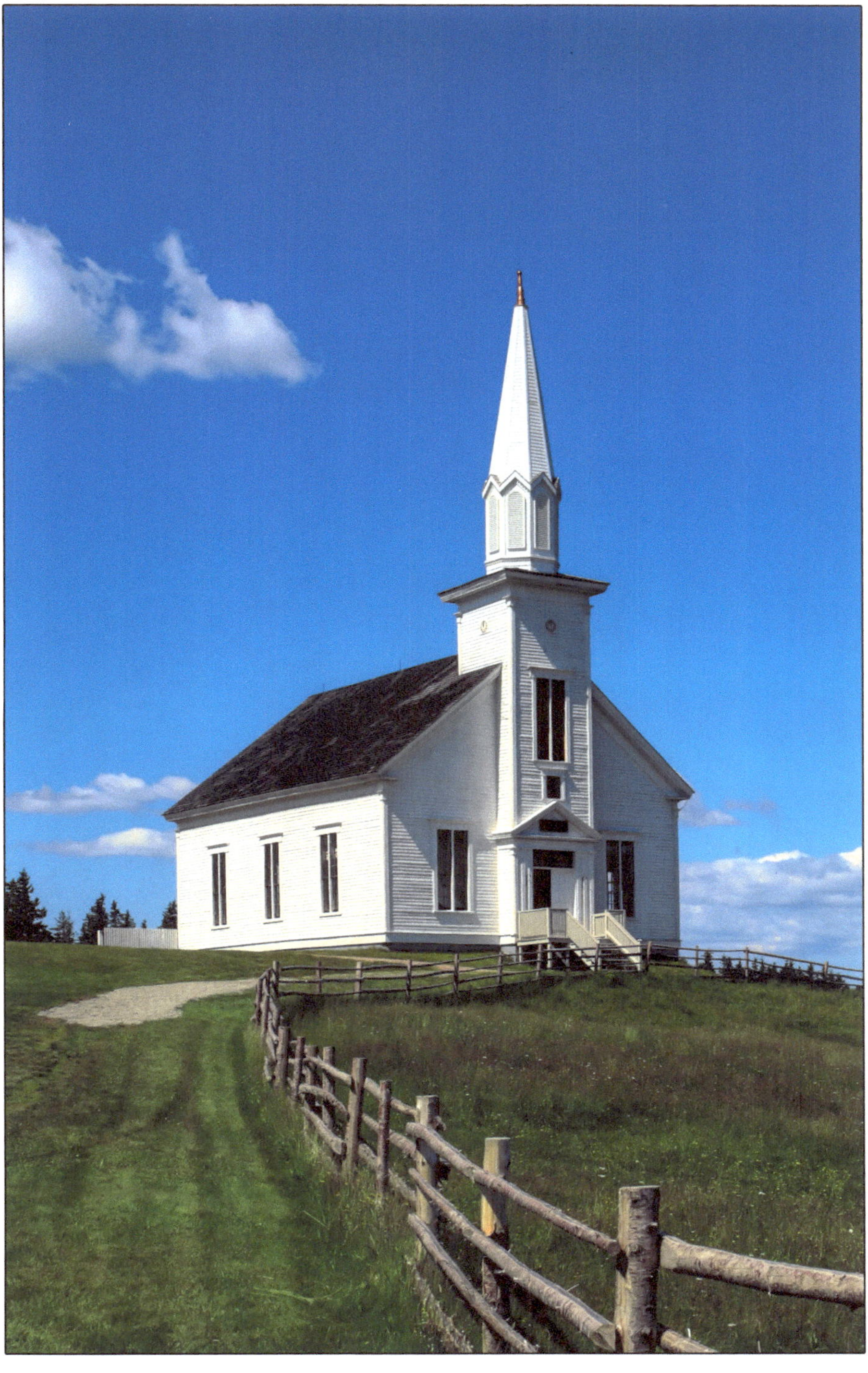

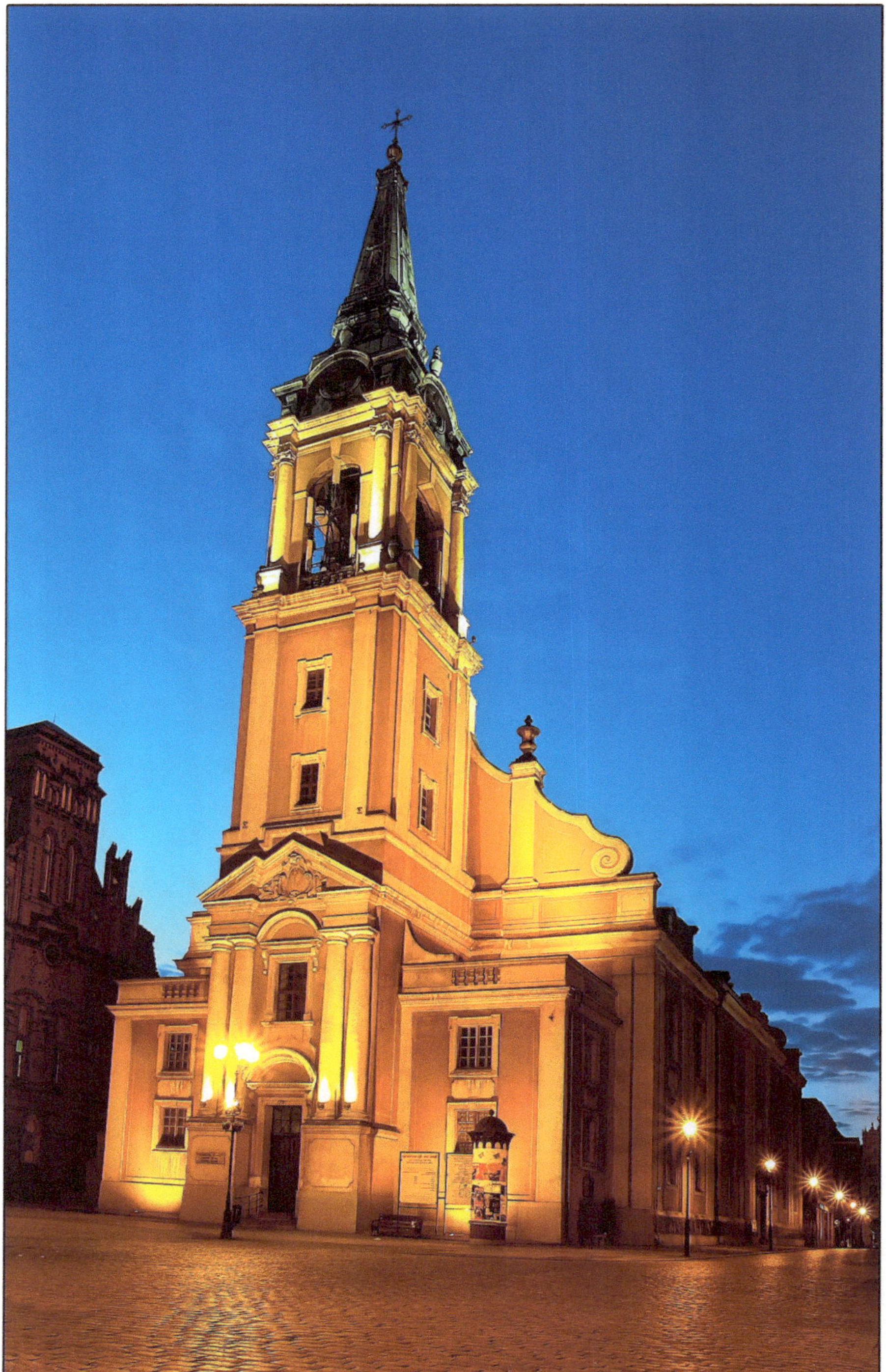

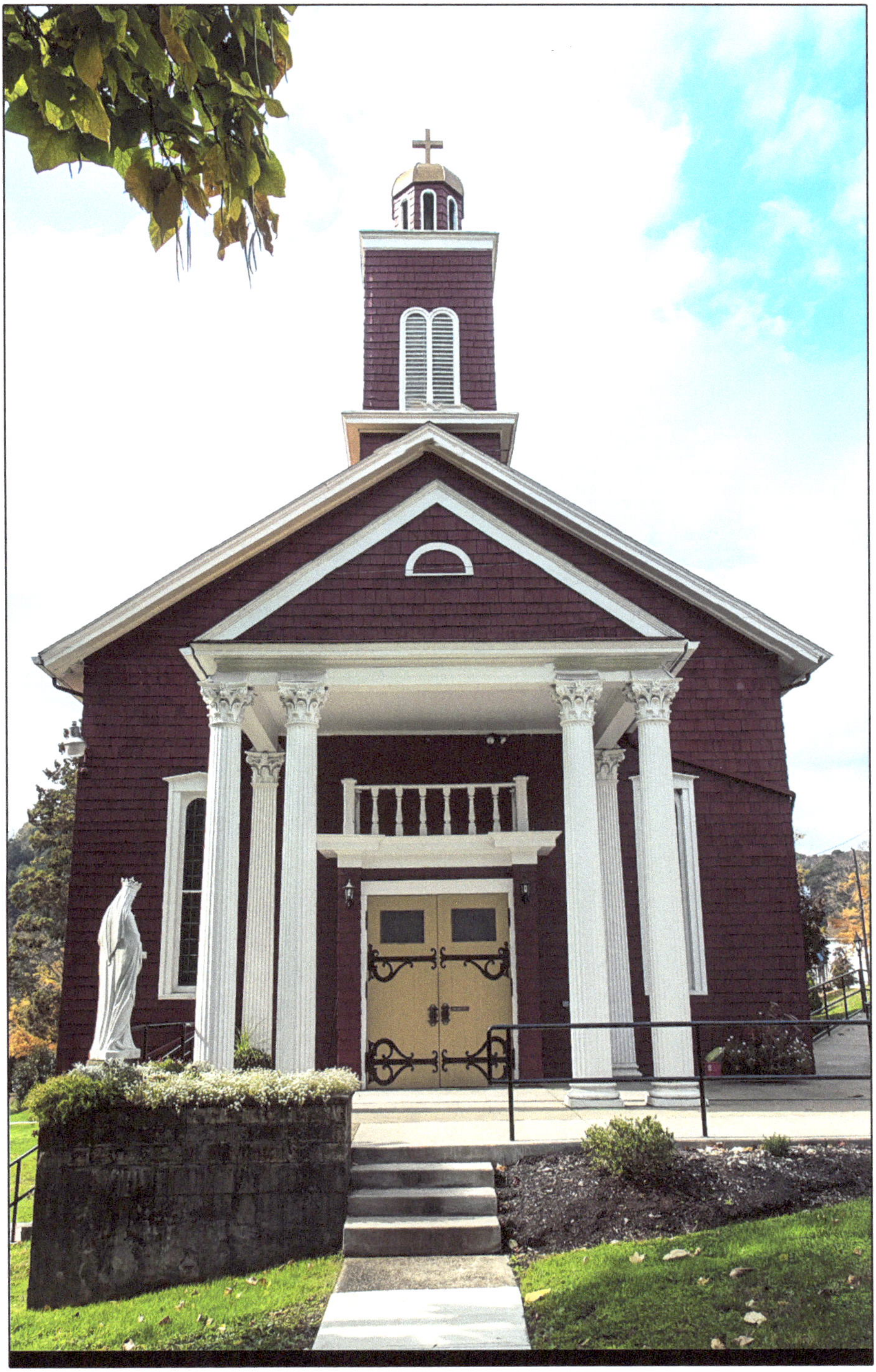

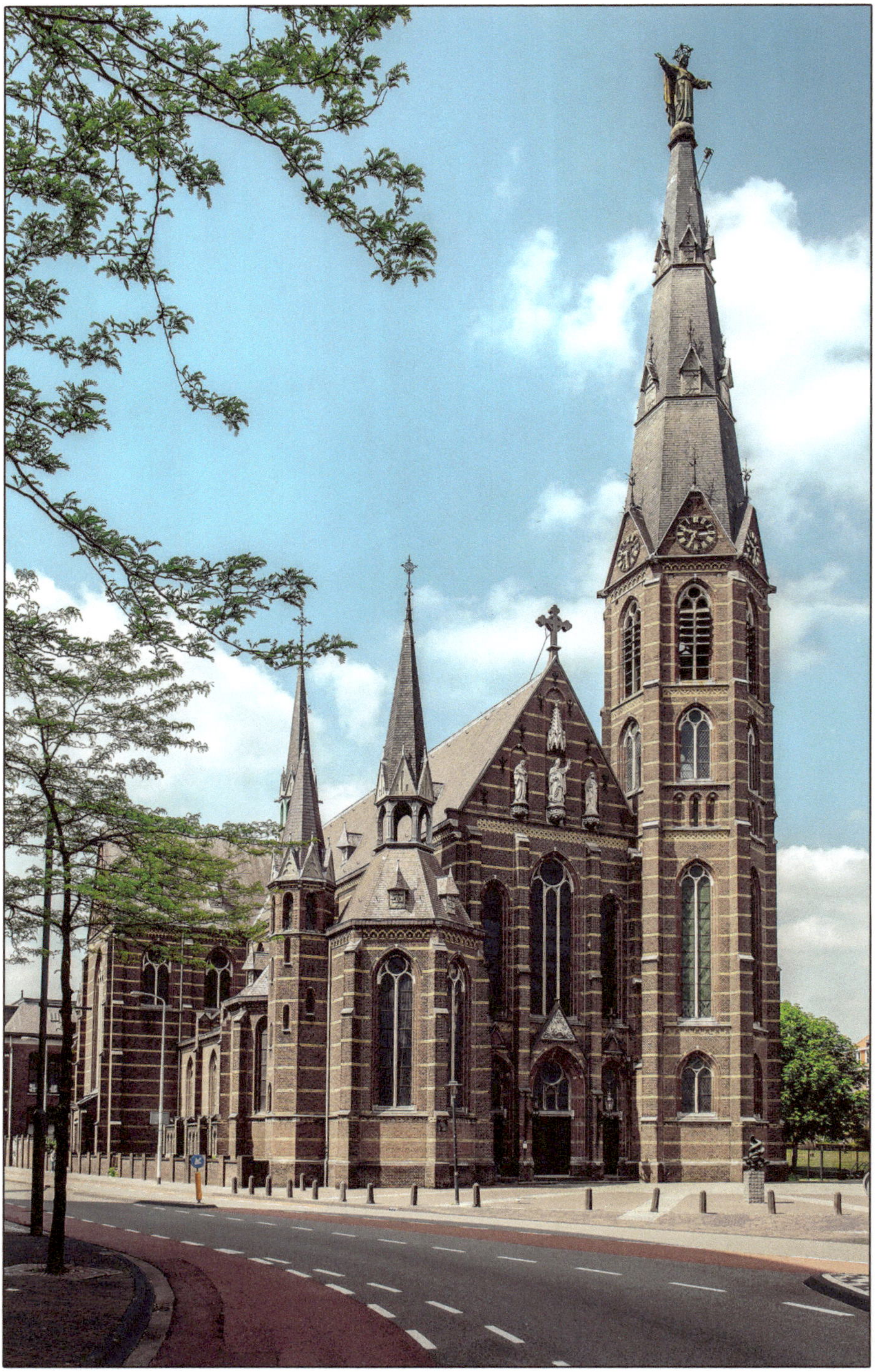

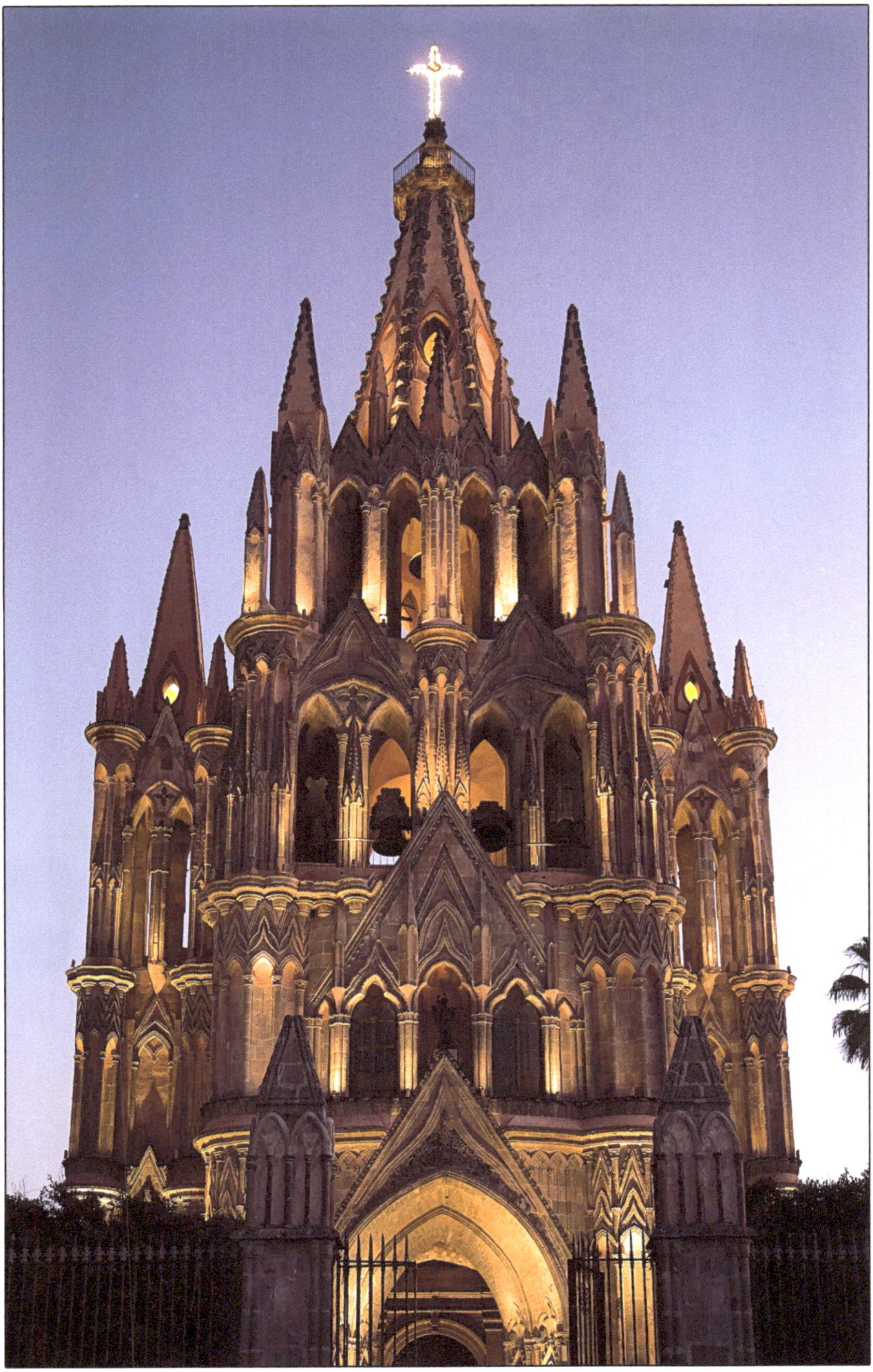

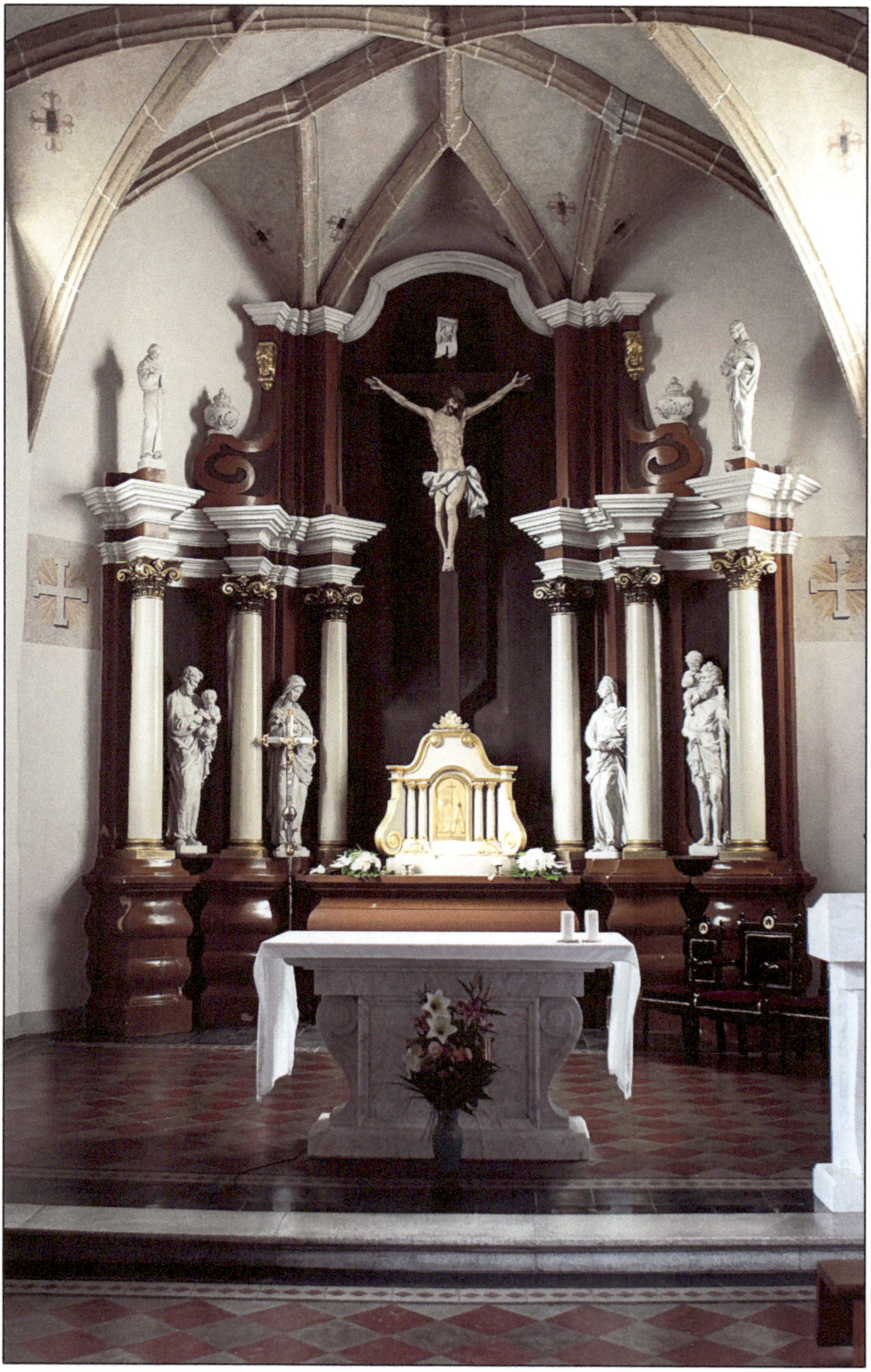

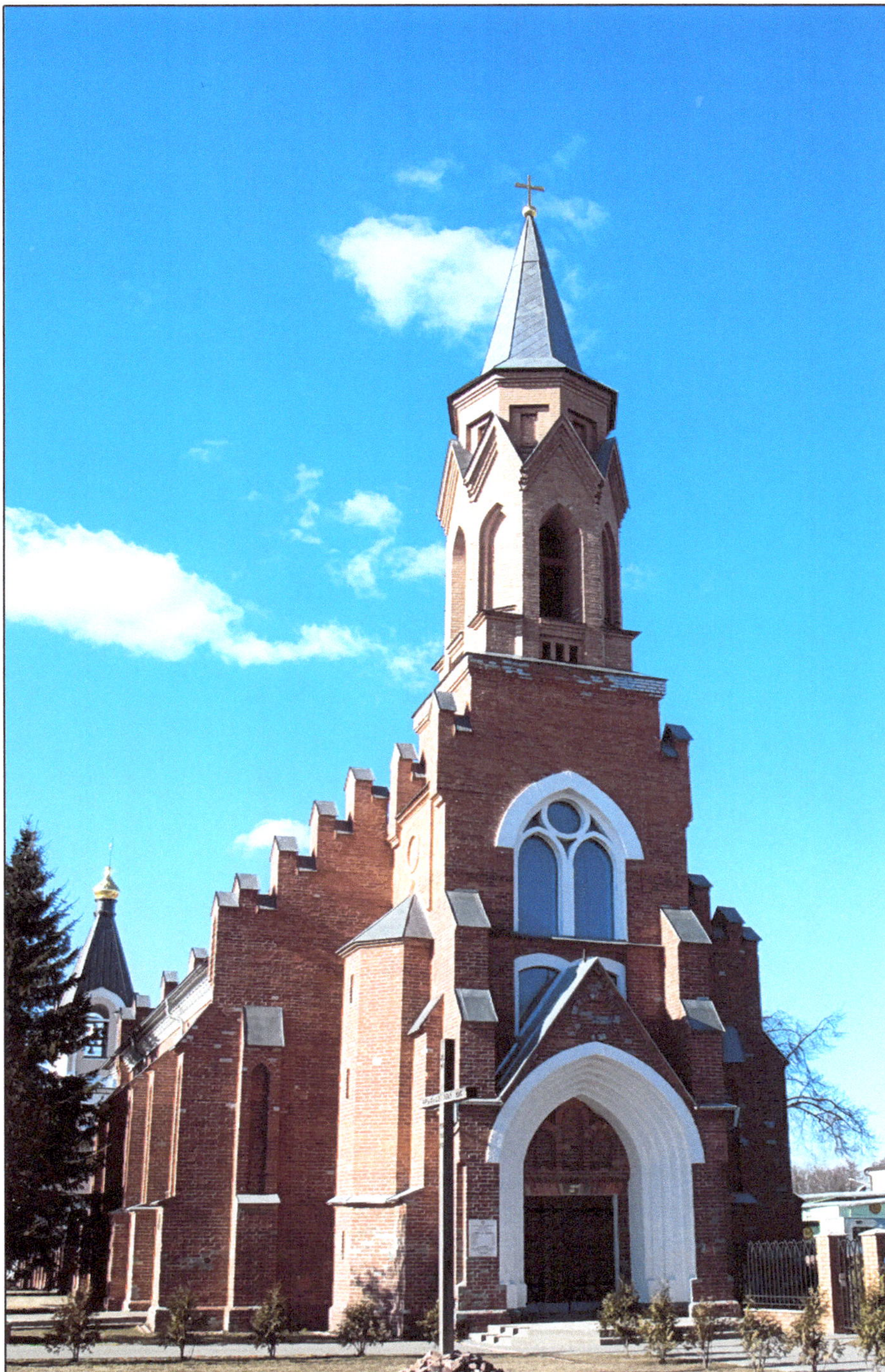

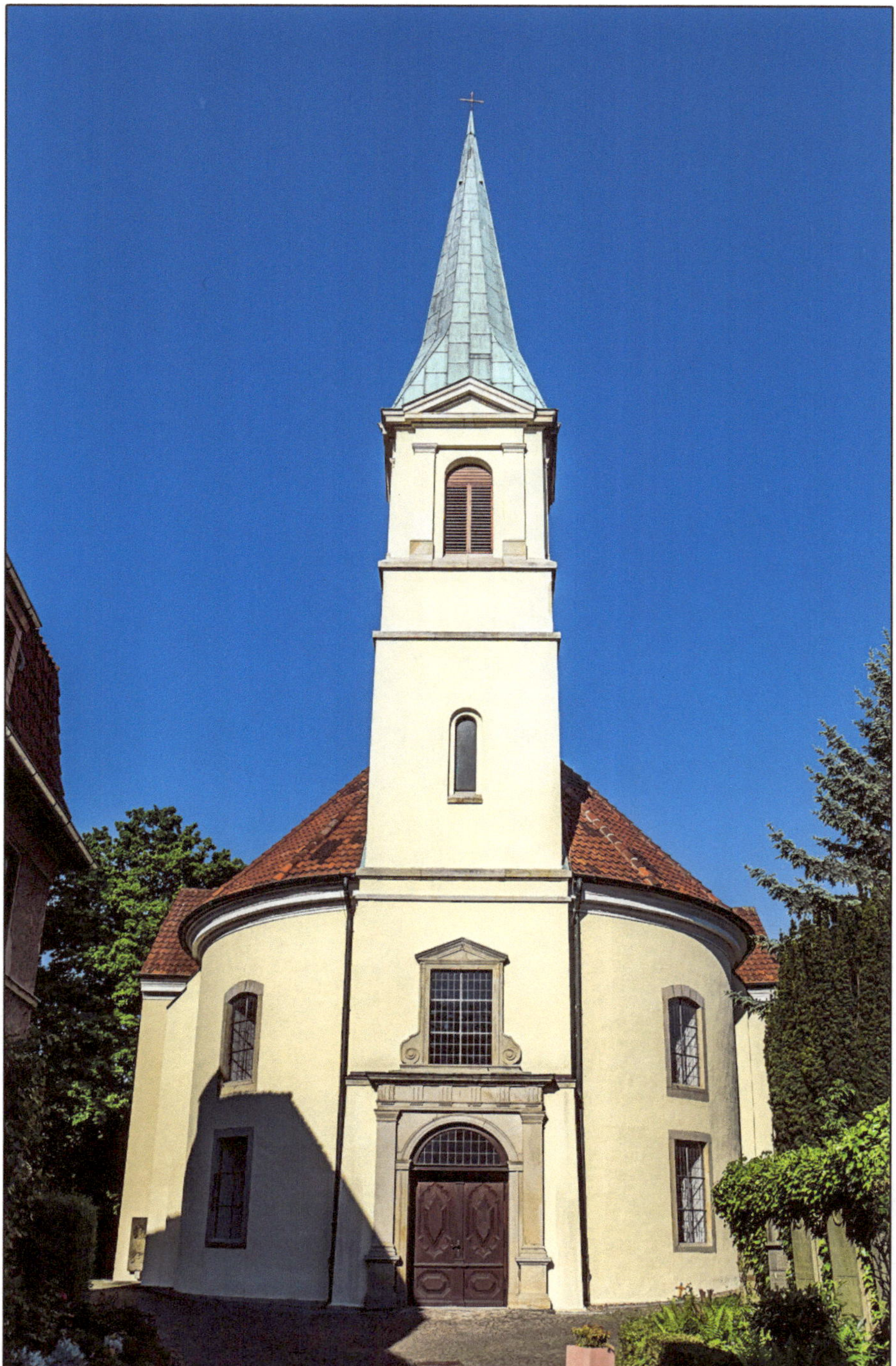

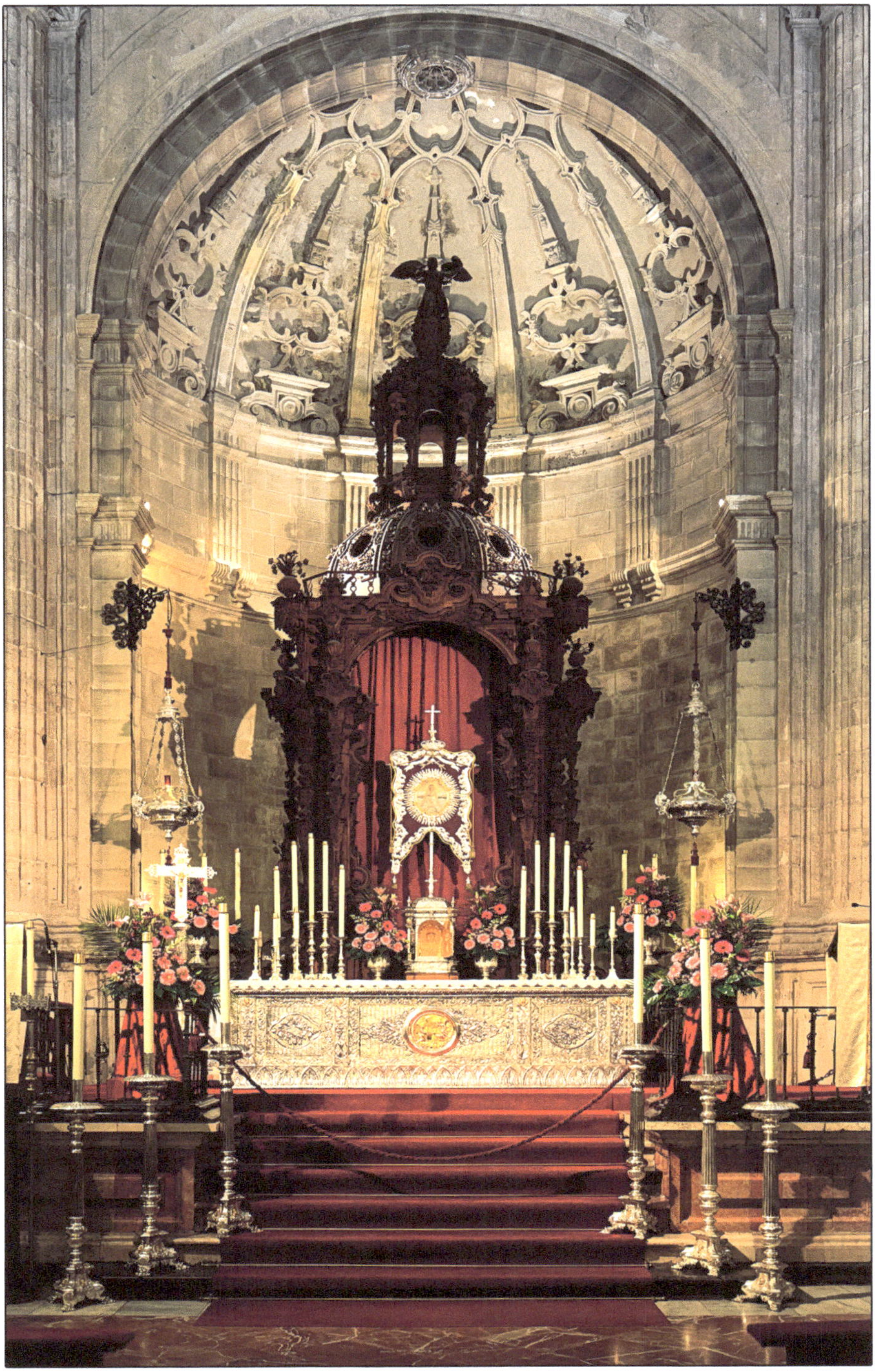

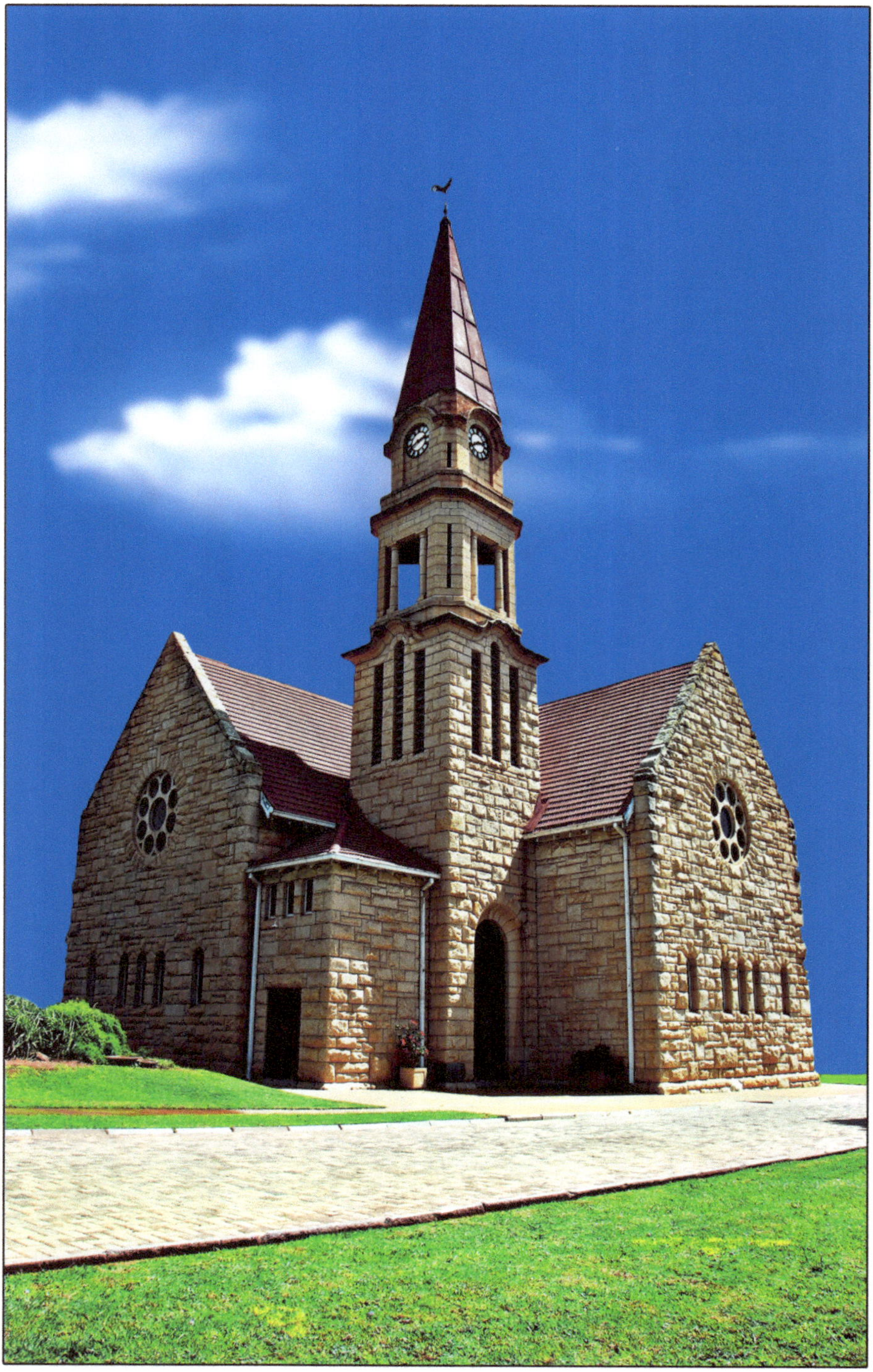

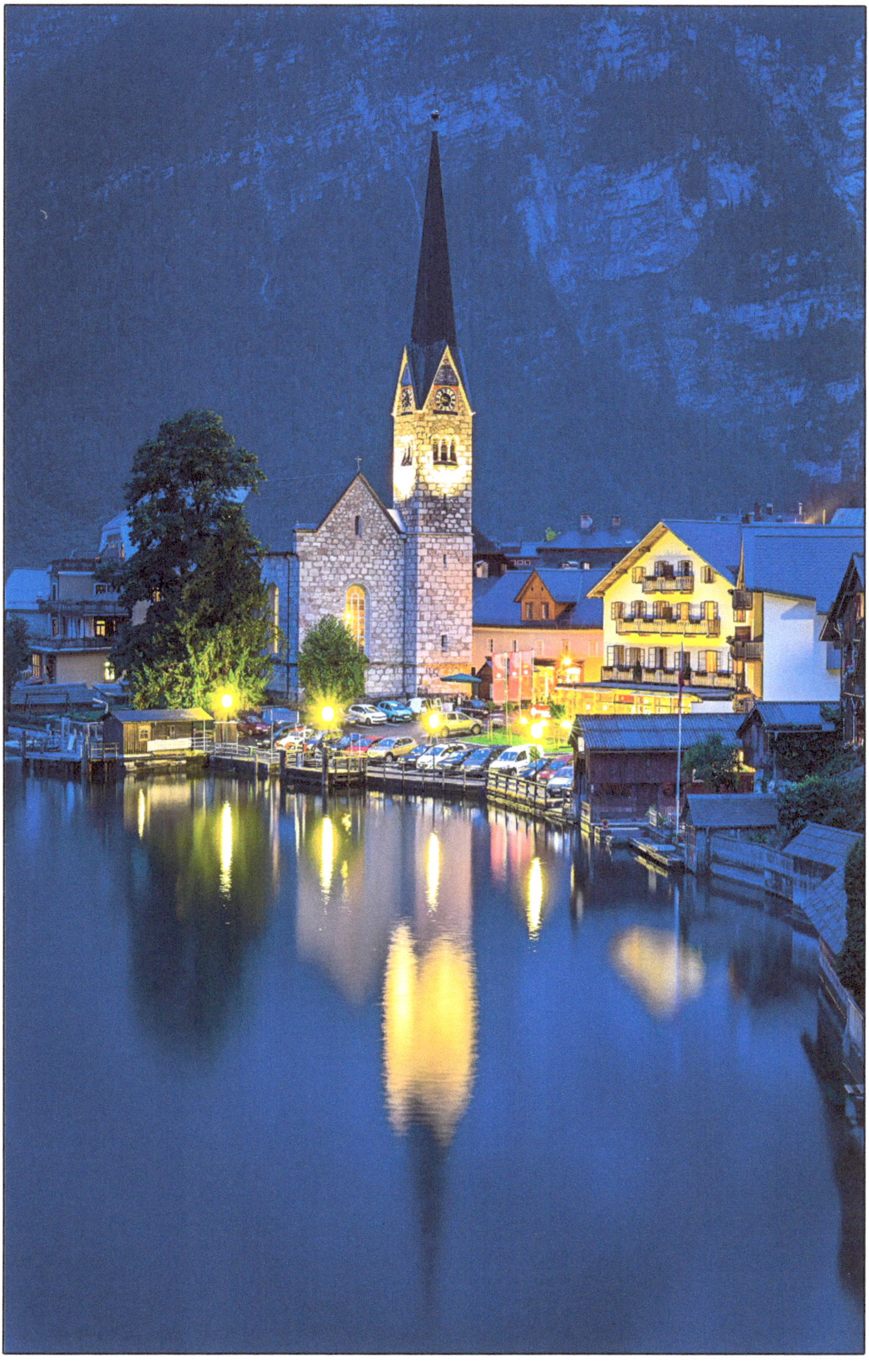

CPSIA information can be obtained
at www.ICGtesting.com
Printed in the USA
LVHW071501070922
727798LV00001B/19
* 9 7 8 1 6 9 7 9 1 4 9 4 8 *